THE HISTORY OF WEATHER

THE HISTORY OF WEATHER

JAMES THAXTER WILLIAMS

Nova Science Publishers, Inc.
Commack, New York

Editorial Production: Susan Boriotti
Office Manager: Annette Hellinger
Graphics: Frank Grucci and John T'Lustachowski
Information Editor: Tatiana Shohov
Book Production: Donna Dennis, Patrick Davin, Christine Mathosian
and Tammy Sauter
Circulation: Maryanne Schmidt
Marketing/Sales: Cathy DeGregory

Library of Congress Cataloging-in-Publication Data

Williams, James Thaxter
    The history of weather / by James Thaxter Williams
            p.   cm.
    Includes bibliographical references and index.
    ISBN 1-56072-622-9
    1. Meteorology--History. 2. Weather--History. I. Title.
QC855.W55   1998   98-40853
551.5'09--dc21   CIP

Copyright © 1999 by Nova Science Publishers, Inc.
    6080 Jericho Turnpike, Suite 207
    Commack, New York 11725
    Tele. 516-499-3103   Fax 516-499-3146
    e-mail: Novascience@earthlink.net
    e-mail: Novascil@aol.com
    Web Site: http://www.nexusworld.com/nova

Printed in the United States of America

Permit me to extend my everlasting thanks to the one person who never doubted that I could do it -- who urged me forward during periods of lethargy and indolence -- who consoled me during anguished bouts of vacillation and self-doubt -- who spurred me to the completion (at last) of my self-imposed chore: writing the (partial) *"History of Weather."*

CONTENTS

Wherein we follow the adventures of early humans as they migrated out of Africa and into Eurasia where for a million years they suffered, endured and survived erratic changes in climate that molded their abilities to not only adapt and prevail but to continue to evolve and acquire social skills that allowed them to exploit natural resources and ultimately develop agriculture and civilization.

Wherein we glimpse a new order of civilization. While other cultures submitted and suffered in a world diverging ever farther from reality, the Greeks embraced an energetic enthusiasm for life and nourished a new, quite different, perspective -- a supremacy of mind in the affairs of men that led to speculations on the meaning of life and the nature of the earth and efforts to provide physical explanations for natural phenomena. Through the power of pure reasoning, they advanced the physical understanding of medicine, mathematics, astronomy, physics and meteorology far beyond previous experience.

Wherein we describe the tools, instruments and machines used to measure weather parameters -- and the renaissance and post-renaissance luminaries that invented them.

Wherein we see 18th century scientists, using the instruments invented in the 17th century, develop the physical laws that 19th century scientists would apply to the atmosphere and lay the theoretical foundations for modern, 20th century, meteorological science.

Wherein we describe the development and early applications of "synoptic" meteorology and "art" of forecasting.

CHAPTER NINE -- THE THEORY OF METEOROLOGY   75

Wherein we unfold the history of meteorological theory. Here we see atmospheric scientists of the 19th and early 20th centuries utilize the increased frequency and accuracy of meteorological observation, in particular that of the upper air, and apply physical laws developed in the17th and 18th century to the atmosphere to provide the theoretical foundations of modern meteorological science. We further document the development and early applications of "synoptic" meteorology and chronicle the introduction of "air-mass/frontal" theory of meteorology.

CHAPTER TEN -- INTO THE 20TH CENTURY   95

Wherein we unfold the history of early 20th century atmospheric scientists as they advance the theoretical knowledge of meteorology by applying the physical laws and theory developed in the 19th century. We chronicle meteorology's second revolution following World War II wherein atmospheric scientists utilize new instruments along with the increased frequency and accuracy of upper air observation to advance theoretical meteorology and improve forecast accuracy.

CHAPTER ELEVEN -- THE NEW METEOROLOGY   103

Wherein we continue to unfold the history of mid-20th century atmospheric scientists as they further advance the theoretical knowledge of meteorology. We follow meteorology's second revolution wherein atmospheric scientists utilize new instruments to advance theoretical meteorology and improve forecast accuracy. Additionally, we chronicle the marriage of theory with the computer, an experiment that ultimately produced modern numerical forecasts whose timeliness and accuracy far exceeds those produced by humans.

CHAPTER TWELVE -- THE HISTORY OF CLIMATE   115

Wherein we chronicle the climate of earth over the eons as it changes with the development and drift of the continents, the rise of huge mountain changes and variations in solar radiance. We further note the development of weather lore, the first form of climatology, by primitive Man and its subsequent refinement over the ages -- and our recent concern over climate changes from industrial pollution.

PREFACE

"Weather is one of the common denominators of our lives. It helps shape our culture, character, conduct, and health. It frequents the pages of our history and can change its course. It colors our conversations, folklore, and literature; it rains on our parades, awes us with its power and beauty, frightens us and sometimes kills us."

-- Weatherwise Magazine

Because meteorology, climate, and weather all refer to activities of the atmosphere, the distinction between the three frequently becomes blurred.

Meteorology deals primarily with dynamic phenomena occurring within the atmosphere -- the changes in the chemistry and physical processes wrought, primarily, by daily and seasonal differences in radiation from the sun and, secondarily, by interactions with the solid continents, liquid oceans and the biological components of the earth. Secondary interactions include both the influences that continents, oceans and life forms have upon the atmosphere and the influence that atmosphere has upon the earth's surface, oceans and life in general.

According to the method of approach and application, modern meteorology has become subdivided into a very large number of specialized sciences. Meteorological science may apply to any atmosphere, real or imagined -- even those of other worlds. By extension it may even refer to the behavior of gaseous blobs in glactic space.

Weather differs from meteorology in that it usually pertains to the state of the atmosphere in terms of its immediate effects upon biological life and particularly to human life. We define weather in terms of those meteorological elements that affect us most directly -- wind, rain, temperature, humidity, cloudiness, and to a lesser extent, brightness, and visibility.

Residents of Venus might define their weather in terms of skies overcast by dense clouds of methane and ammonia, caustic acid rain and an ambient temperature that would melt lead. Inhabitants of Mars would speak of clear skies and brittle cold interrupted only by howling dust storms. Meteorology prevails throughout the universe. Weather, a human invention, exists, as far as we know, only on earth.

Whereas weather refers to real-time, usually short-term (minutes to months) variations of the atmosphere, climatology concerns itself with long-term (decades to millennia) averages of the various weather parameters with an eye towards comparison of present, past and future weather regimes.

The *Guinness Book of Weather Facts and Feats* describes climate as the "average weather condition of a particular part of the world." C. S. Durst calls climate "the synthesis of the weather." The *Glossary of Meteorology* defines the climate of a specified area as "the statistical collective of its weather conditions during a specified interval of time (usually several decades)."

Definable types of climate exist only because the influence of the sun, the seas, and the land contours establishes a climate regime a normal range of weather conditions beyond which the weather rarely if ever departs.

Distance from the equator (latitude) determines the primary climate of a region. Altitude above sea level, however, greatly modifies the latitudinal climate while available moisture combined with temperature (and/or altitude) determines the type of vegetation that grows in a given area. Climatologists also make a distinction between the general or macroclimate, the local or mesoclimate, and the small-scale or microclimate. Seasons, of course, contribute substantial variety to the weather and climate of any locality -- although seasonal effects diminish in the tropics.

Climatology, the long-term manifestation of weather, generally hews more closely to the definition of weather than of meteorology. Since the middle of the 20th century, however, the domain of climatology has expanded to include a broad cross-section of traditional science. Physicists, chemists, mathematicians, statisticians, oceanographers, geologists, archeologists and radiologists spring to mind as some of the disciplines other than meteorology now actively involved in climatological research.

METEOROLOGY, CLIMATE AND WEATHER

The Glossary of Meteorology, published by the American Meteorological Society, provides the following definitions of meteorology, climate, and weather.

METEOROLOGY

The study dealing with the phenomena of the **atmosphere**. This includes not only the physics, chemistry, and dynamics of the atmosphere, but is extended to include many of the direct effects of the atmosphere upon the earth's surface, the oceans, and life in general. The goals often ascribed to meteorology are the complete understanding, accurate prediction, and artificial control of atmosphere phenomena.

Meteorology may be subdivided, according to the methods of approach and the applications to human activities, into a large number of specialized sciences.

A distinction can be drawn between meteorology and **climatology**, the latter being primarily concerned with average, not actual, weather conditions. Meteorology may be subdivided, according to the methods of approach and the applications to human activities, into a large number of specialized sciences.

CLIMATOLOGY

The long-term manifestations of **weather**, however they may be expressed. More rigorously, the climate of a specified area is represented by the statistical collective of its weather conditions during a specified interval of time (usually several decades).

Definable types of climate exist only because the sun's influence, the seas, and the land contours are sufficiently regular and permanent always to bring weather back toward the normal for the season after temporary departures. The effects of these **climate controls** led to a basic climatic classification into such as 'Arctic,' 'marine,' 'mountain,' etc. Distinction is also made between the general or **macroclimate**, the local or **mesoclimate**, and the small-scale or **microclimate**.

WEATHER

The state of the **atmosphere**, mainly with respect to its effects upon life and human activities. As distinguished from **climate**, weather consists of the short-term (minutes to months) variations of the atmosphere. Popularly, weather is thought of in terms of temperature, humidity, precipitation, cloudiness, brightness, visibility, and wind. . . .

INTRODUCTION

Geophysicists have recently revised Earth's geological history. In the latest version, based on the newly developed theory of plate tectonics, our earth appears as a dynamic, pulsating, living body whose animated past features shifting continents, disappearing oceans, changes in atmospheric composition, growing and disintegrating mountain chains, severe climate fluctuations, and mass extinctions of existing life.

In just the last few decades, scientists have determined the underlying cause of these mighty convulsions. A few miles beneath the solid surface upon which we live, a slowly churning layer of mushy rock, called the asthenosphere, maintains the earth in a state of constant agitation. The continuous stirring of the asthenosphere breaks the earth's thin crust into slabs of various sizes called tectonic plates, upon which rest our familiar continents. Floating on the gently-boiling plastic rock, these huge lithospheric plates drift around the world. Moving at a rate of only a few centimeters a year (perhaps four or five inches during the span of a human life), they collide, coalesce, and re-fragment. As they do, they generate volcanoes, earthquakes, and, most disruptive of all, Ice Ages.

Violent upheavals such as earthquakes and volcanoes occur in isolated episodes of limited scope. Ice ages have global repercussions with profound consequences for all living organisms. In past eras, immense sheets of ice covered as much as one-third of the earth's land surface. As they grew and spread toward the equator, they compressed livable space into increasingly narrow bands, encroaching upon and destroying local habitats. Creatures, dependent on a particular environment, had to migrate with the shifting climate or adapt to new conditions -- or perish. More than once in the last 3.5 billion years climate changes have eliminated all but a small fraction of Earth's plant and animal life.

About 65 million years ago, the immense land masses of Antarctica, Siberia, and North America drifted beneath the poles. Because continents hold less heat than oceans, the earth's heat budget changed and temperatures dropped. Ice and snow accumulating near the poles reflected sunlight back into space, lowering the temperature even further. Fifteen million years ago glaciers formed in Antarctica. Seven million years ago the great Northern Hemisphere ice sheet began to grow. The Pleistocene Ice Age, in which we currently dwell, began about two million years ago.

Coincidentally, our human species evolved against this backdrop of ice. Since the appearance of hominids on earth three to four million years ago, glaciers have spread deep into the middle latitudes of Europe and North America on numerous occasions. Only 18 thousand years ago glaciers blanketed much of Europe and, in North America, spread into territories now called Indiana, Ohio, and Pennsylvania.

Ice Ages have profound effects on living organisms but our evolving, pre-human, ancestors adapted well. They developed both physical and behavioral flexibility which led to larger brains, bi-pedal locomotion, a refined hand, and ultimately success as the worlds dominant animal species.

Ancient humans hunted, gathered, foraged, and scavenged for their sustenance. The climate, and thus the flora and fauna upon which they depended, determined their location and movements. In many cases they adopted a semi-nomadic style of living, remaining in one place until a depletion of resources dictated a move to a new location.

Climate had a substantial effect on the development of early civilizations. Bountiful tropical climates present little incentive to create advanced civilizations while harsh climates require continuous effort just to survive. Temperate climates combine winter's incentive to improve conditions with summer's abundance, leaving time for social advancement and technological progress.

Weather patterns and weather situations vary from year to year but usually, during the span of a human life, return with some regularly to a median or common set of occurrences that we call the local climate -- "the statistical collective of local weather conditions." If, after a generation or two, the local weather noticeably (measurably) improves or worsens, a change in climate has occurred.

Both biological and geological forces influence and change climate. Tectonic forces move whole continents into different climatic zones. They also build mountains that redirect the atmospheric flow causing local climate to change. Residual dust from volcanoes reflect sunlight and cool the earth.

Subtle variations in ocean temperature can affect distributions of minute sea dwelling organisms. A decline or increase in their population causes changes in the atmospheric composition that, in turn, may induce climate changes. Human activities add chemicals to the air that change the composition of the atmosphere with both short-term and long-term climatic effects.

Biological (short-term) or geological (long-term) influences do not greatly affect day-to-day weather. These forces, however, do gradually change local climates and thus effect changes in local weather regimes. Humans have inadvertently produced local climate changes since they adopted civilization. Whole forests have succumbed to pre-historic pottery industries and soil degradation by human activities has reduced once-thriving communities to bleak emptiness on more occasions than one.

Today, the world frets about global warming -- apparently induced by human activities that have added large concentrations of carbon dioxide and other "greenhouse" gases to the atmosphere -- with its potentially dire, even catastrophic, consequences.

This book, in addition to explaining many of the atmospheric processes we call weather, addresses the profound effect weather and climate has had on human evolution and advancement -- and the profound effect human activities have had on climate and weather. In this sense, it may be called a "history of weather."

Those who find this "history" hopelessly oriented toward a "Western Philosophy" will hopefully find solace in the knowledge that western Europeans and Americans (residents of the United States and Canada) have in fact performed most of the early research leading to today's tangible understanding of meteorological science and the marvels of modern weather observing and forecasting.

CHAPTER ONE

THE BEGINNING

Wherein we describe the earth's fiery birth, its subsequent cooling and gradual modification into a beautiful, essentially benevolent, planet with fortuitous quantities of water and an atmosphere hospitable to earthly life.

"It started with a chaotic, irregular cloud of gas and dust."
-- Carl Sagan

METEOROLOGY OF THE UNIVERSE

Like jewels scattered on a swath of black velvet, uncountable millions of galaxies, each containing uncountable billions of stars, shimmer in the night sky. Some immense; others modest in size, they come in three basic shapes; oval, spherical and, most beautiful by far, flat, gently rotating spirals with delicate outreaching arms.

Some five billion years ago, on the on the fringe of one arm of one such spiral galaxy, there floated a unique fragment of cosmic dust, a remnant of some star that exploded eons before. This ethereal blob of celestial flotsam and jetsam, nearly transparent and quite small by galactic standards, rotated slowly, indicating a concentration of mass near its center. Over time, this point of mass grew at the expense of other, smaller particles in its vicinity -- pulling them in by the force of its gravity.

Eventually the dominant central mass grew so large and dense that its gravitational pull attracted even the outermost particles. The cloud began to contract around the central aggregation. As the cloud shrank, its speed of rotation increased -- like that of a spinning ice skater retracting her arms. The cloud also began to flatten as those particles outside the plane of rotation fell more rapidly inward, adding even more mass to the core. Those particles within the plane of rotation fell less rapidly or, if their speed of rotation matched the inward tug of gravity, did not fall inward at all but remained in orbit about the center.

Friction, from new matter crashing into the ever growing central body, raised the temperature of its interior to a critical state. It began to glow a pale pink. Hydrogen atoms, violently thrown together deep in the interior fused, initiating a thermonuclear chain reaction. The nucleus of this once diaphanous cloud of dust and gas changed from pale pink to bright red then to brilliant white. Suddenly it exploded into flame and became a star -- our sun -- and began to radiate vast amounts of energy back into space.

Several smaller conglomerations of debris that had resisted the inward pull of the central core's gravity -- and avoided collision with other large bodies -- orbited the new sun at random distances from the center. As they continued to sweep up matter in their vicinity, they aggregated impressive bulks of mass. Earth, one survivor of this tumultuous game of chance, continued to grow, gathering in successively larger bits of debris -- rocks, boulders and mountain-size chunks of rock -- and a moon.

THE LAND, AIR AND SEA

The violent process of accumulating material generated incredible heat. The central core of the earth, like that of its sun, grew hotter as its mass increased. Unlike the sun, however, it never gained sufficient mass to generate thermonuclear reactions. But it did grow hot enough to melt the material deep within its central regions. As the core melted, the heavier elements such as iron and nickel gravitated to the center of the planet, while the lighter elements such as silicon and carbon floated toward the surface. Many lighter elements arrived at the surface in the form of gas which formed an atmosphere composed of, among other things, water vapor, carbon dioxide and methane.

Clouds, ten miles thick, formed in the new blanket of air. The thick layer of cloud prevented sunlight from reaching the surface, but carbon dioxide and water vapor within the cloud prevented the earth from radiating its heat into space. Rain fell but the surface, which remained blistering hot, immediately re-evaporated the water.

Pressure from the outer layers and decay of radioactive materials within continued to generate tremendous heat at the center of the globe. Unable to lose the heat by radiating it into space, the earth began to glow a dull red and suddenly -- dramatically -- melted. As the earth liquefied, gravity pulled the once irregular ball of aggregate into a nearly perfect spherical drop composed of molten rock floating on a core of liquid metal.

The intense surface heat blasted the entire proto-atmosphere into space and, its fever broken, the earth began to cool. Fragile islands of rock formed, thickened and hardened in the vast sea of molten lava. As they floated about, some smashed together to form larger land masses and eventually to assemble huge continents. Meanwhile, a second atmosphere formed from water vapor and other gases escaping from the interior.

For a long time Earth's blazing hot surface maintained very high atmospheric temperatures. The large concentrations of water vapor and carbon dioxide in the new atmosphere trapped the earth's heat. Although the surface temperature hovered between 140°F and 200°F, temperatures were cooler at higher levels and water vapor condensed into a deep blanket of cloud that shrouded the entire earth. Rain fell continuously from the dense cloud layer but, as before, could not reach the surface before re-evaporating in the extreme heat.

Ever so slowly the earth cooled. In time, rain began to fall upon the crusts of the newly formed surface. Convective thunderstorms raged continuously as endless wind and rain weathered away the highlands. Rivers carried vast amounts of water, laden with minerals captured from the land, into the lower basins to form lakes and oceans.

Hot gases from the earth's interior, saturated with minerals and nutrients, spewed forth from underwater volcanoes and cracks in the sea floor. Nutrients from the land and sea and catalytic heat from the sun and volcanic outpourings generated a rich broth of highly complex nucleic acids, sugars, phosphates and proteins. These nutrients, suitable for the development of primitive forms of life, accumulated in the shallow reaches of the seas and lakes. After a billion years in the throes of birth, Earth, replete with resources, sat primed for the advent of life.

EARLY LIFE

During the million-year rainstorm, a primordial soup, stocked with raw chemicals, minerals, and simple molecules, formed in the ancient seas. The exact process by which life emerged from this reservoir of primeval elements remains forever a mystery. Theories, however, abound.

By some accounts, the virtually continuous lightning discharges through the murky cloud banks of the archaic atmosphere generated proteins and simple molecules which fell to the surface and accumulated in the oceans. Chemical reactions within this vast well of inorganic substances forged the pre-biotic molecules into more complex nucleic acids, sugars, phosphates, and proteins which form the building blocks of life.

Volcanic activity occurred much more frequently three and a half billion years ago. Perhaps nutrients and the catalytic heat necessary to produce life from proteins and other organic precursors occurred in the vicinity of volcanic outpourings on the ocean floor. Even today such vents exist where moving tectonic plates have separated the ocean floor. Sea water seeping into crevices in the earth's crust, heats up, and resurfaces brimming with minerals. These self-renewing factories of chemicals and nutrients stimulate and support oases of life sustained by heat from subterranean sources rather than sunlight.

Exactly when or how the first living cell arose remains the subject of intense study -- and debate. Somehow sequences of chemical reactions, catalyzed by ultraviolet radiation from the sun or intense heat from the oceans, converted simpler organic molecules into ever more complex structures. In time, primitive single-celled creatures (called prokaryotes) developed from the organic molecules. They had no nucleus and reproduced by simple cell division -- but they claim the distinction of being Earth's first form of life.

A CHANGE IN THE ATMOSPHERE

The ancient atmosphere contained an abundance of carbon dioxide but very little free oxygen. This combination, while inhospitable to most modern life forms, corresponded exactly to the requirements for the formation and development of life.

Oxygen, then as now a dangerously corrosive and poisonous gas, reacted violently with nearly everything it touched. As fast as it formed, it combined with minerals in the soil, rocks, and water allowing little or no free oxygen or ozone to accumulate in the atmosphere. The concentration of oxygen that exists today would have destroyed embryonic forms of primal life as fast as they occurred.

The large concentrations of carbon dioxide, a "greenhouse gas," trapped the earth's heat close to the surface maintaining very high atmospheric and oceanic temperatures -- possibly as high as 140°F. This extreme heat, while adding another catalyst to the process of life formation, also prevented life from evolving beyond simple one-celled algae or bacteria.

A billion years after the first living creatures evolved, the earth finally cooled to the point where the dense cloud cover could thin and break up and the rains could cease. The sun began finally to shine upon the earth's surface providing conditions for the second great leap in the development of life on earth -- photosynthesis.

Without sunlight, early life forms subsisted by scavenging nutrients and minerals from the water and producing sugar for energy through fermentation. After the clouds parted and the sun appeared, one species of blue-green bacteria (cyanobacteria) learned to use sunlight to split molecules of water and carbon dioxide to make energy-rich glucose -- emitting oxygen in the (photosynthetic) process.

Five hundred million years later the earth abounded with cyanobacteria, an organism able to build its own food from small molecules using carbon dioxide from the air and energy from the sun. Having no natural enemies, the cyanobacteria population grew unbounded. However, the excessive quantities of oxygen they produced poisoned the atmosphere for existing life forms, including the cyanobacteria itself.

As the oxygen increased, the bacteria expired or retreated into environments where oxygen could not reach. They had succeeded so spectacularly that they upset the oxygen-carbon dioxide balance and destroyed their natural habitat -- and forever altered the conditions of evolution.

A New Atmosphere -- New Life Forms

The biosphere, born of the lithosphere, the hydrosphere, and the atmosphere became and remains an integral sphere of influence in the earth's dynamic processes.

Atmospheric changes wrought by the blue-green algae primed the ancient environment for more complex life forms. As oxygen increased and carbon dioxide decreased, life forms evolved in response. At first the newly evolved organisms could merely tolerate the increased oxygen. Later versions, however, increased their food-gathering efficiency by actively employing oxygen in their metabolism.

Thus began a billion years of symbiotic interrelationship between animals that used oxygen and gave off carbon dioxide, and plants that consumed carbon dioxide and respired oxygen. A layer of ozone, a different form of oxygen that filters out much of the sun's harmful ultraviolet radiation, formed high in the stratosphere, producing a more hospitable environment for life.

The decrease in carbon dioxide permitted the earth to cool to more tolerable levels. After another billion years, an advanced form of cell life evolved -- the eukaryotic or "nucleated" cell -- based on photosynthesis and the abundance of oxygen provided by their prokaryotic ancestors. The eukaryote nucleus contained genetic material which allowed parents to pass physical improvements to their offspring, allowing new variations of eukaryotes to arise and diversify.

The rapid growth and diversification of the more efficient eukaryote cells marked the beginning of the Cambrian period, an age of specialization, regulation, organization, and differentiation in size and complexity. Geologists and paleontologists refer to this period of geological time --beginning about 550 million years ago -- as the Phanerozoic era, the era of manifest life.

Without exception, eukaryotic cells compose the more complex, specialized multi-cellular forms of life. However their very complexity makes them exceedingly vulnerable to changes in environment and climate.

The more advanced the organism the more dependent it becomes upon stable conditions. Earth, however, does not constitute a stable life-support system. Several times over the past 550 million years environmental catastrophes have destroyed nearly all eukaryote forms of life -- while the resilient bacteria go about their business relatively undisturbed.

CHAPTER TWO

NOMADIC CONTINENTS

Wherein we discuss the interacting dynamics of Earth's four physical spheres -- the atmosphere, the hydrosphere, the lithosphere and the biosphere -- how they evolved in concert and remain in balance through a system of symbiotic geo-chemical interchanges maintained by the constant stirrings of the lithosphere.

"We have within our grasp a new concept to aid our understanding of the earth's dynamics: the idea that rocks can evolve."
-- Peter Westbroek

TECTONIC PLATES

Between the earth's molten metallic core and the lithosphere, Earth's thin surface crust upon which we dwell, lies the asthenosphere, a slowly churning "mantle" of plastic rock. Heat from the center of the earth keeps the asthenosphere percolating. This slow-motion boil, with heated magma rising in one sector and sinking elsewhere, has caused the lithosphere to break into some 20 odd slabs called tectonic plates. These large 60 mile thick plates float on the asthenosphere and, as they drift around the world, gradually move the continents into new land-sea configurations.

When one plate bumps into another, the heavier plate sinks which forces the lighter one to rise. At the same time, some of the surface material from the sinking plate gets scraped off onto the surface of the over-riding plate -- a process that creates mountain chains and causes earthquakes. The sinking plate melts when it reaches the intense heat of the mantle but eventually resurfaces as volcanic gas and igneous rock. Sometimes scientists use the term "tectonics" to include both the dynamic workings of the asthenosphere and the consequent recycling of the lithosphere.

A German meteorologist, Alfred Wegener, first advanced the revolutionary concept of "continental drift" in 1912 after noting the congruency of the African and South American coasts. A man of great vision and tenacity, he generated persuasive geological evidence to illustrate that all the continents once were joined. The theory gathered few converts, however, because no one could envision a mechanism for moving continents.

After World War II, oceanographers discovered the Great Atlantic Ridge, part of a submerged mountain chain 44,000 miles long that wraps around the earth like seams on a baseball. Eventually, scientists realized that this ridge marks the line where tectonic plates separate allowing molten rock and gases to gush out. Additional evidence, based on measurements of ocean floor spreading, led ultimately to general acceptance of plate tectonic theory and reinstated Wegener's status as a visionary scientist.

The discovery that continents, riding on huge portions of the earth's crust, move, collide, grow, fragment and disperse answers many long-standing geological questions. Tectonics provides a logical reason for volcanoes and earthquakes and explains how ancient seafloors arrived on mountain tops thousands of feet high. And (again, previously suggested by Wegener) it solves, at least partially, the riddle of Ice Age Climates.

THE ROCKS OF LIFE

The development and expansion of tectonic theory also led to the concept of a physically dynamic earth composed of four physical spheres of activity -- the atmosphere, the hydrosphere, the lithosphere and the biosphere. These four basic components of the earth evolved over the eons in a tumultuous interactive thermo-geo-chemical concert. The processes continue, albeit very slowly, and now remain in unsteady balance through a system of symbiotic interchanges maintained by the constant stirrings of the tectonicsphere.

The biosphere, created from components of the lithosphere, maintains its existence by exploiting the lithosphere through means of hydrospheric and the atmospheric activity. The transactions involve chemistry, hydrodynamics, fluid mechanics and a number of other arcane physical processes. In all, six complex cycles of exchange occur jointly between the four spheres. Exchanges involving the lithosphere progress very slowly while the three taking place between the atmosphere, the hydrosphere and the biosphere proceed relatively fast. The interchanges involve chemistry, hydrodynamics, fluid mechanics and other arcane physical processes.

The atmosphere uses hygroscopic (water attracting) nuclei -- plant spoors, dust from the land, chemicals expired by marine life and salt particles produced by interaction of the oceans and the air to attract water vapor. Gradually the nuclei grow into water droplets which form clouds and produce rain.

Atmospheric forces drive storms -- rain, wind, and freezing temperatures -- over the land where they weather away the lithosphere and release minerals into the soil and gases into the atmosphere. The biosphere uses minerals from the soil and gases (primarily oxygen and carbon dioxide) from the atmosphere to sustain plant and animal life. Rivers transport organic minerals from biospheric by-products and non-organic materials from the lithosphere to the hydrosphere. These minerals, excepting those consumed by marine life, settle to the ocean floor forming thick layers of sediment which eventually harden into rock (lithify). Marine life, as it dies and falls to the ocean floor, contributes additional sediment. Moving pieces of the lithosphere transport the oceanic sedimentary rock back to the surface either as uplifted mountains, volcanic gas and dust or molten rock.

Thus, the lithosphere, the atmosphere, the biosphere and the hydrosphere form a complex, symbiotic loop that continuously recycles minerals and nutrients necessary to maintain Earth's life. The biosphere, the most important sphere from our perspective, could not exist without the concurrent inter-active relationship with the other three. Over the next few billion years, the earth will continue to cool and the motions of the tectonicsphere will slow. As it does, life on earth will gradually de-evolve into ever simpler creatures and eventually disappear.

CHAPTER THREE

ICE AGES AND THE ASCENT OF MAN

Wherein we chronicle the drift of continents and discuss their role in glacial development over the eons which, in turn, affected the development of Man as he learned to survive, prosper and populate the world in an age of ice, ultimately to emerge as Earth's dominant life form.

"There can be little doubt that the great technical ingenuity man has displayed over the last 5000 years is a heritage from past ice ages. To have survived the fearsome conditions of those years our distance ancestors had to be both extremely hardy and very clever."
-- Sir Fred Hoyle

MOTHER NATURE

Customarily we regard Mother Nature as the magnanimous overseer of Earth's well-being, exercising protective care of the environment. We script Nature as wondrous and munificent and place humans in the role of callous, desecrating opportunists, laying waste to the planet.

Possible this sanguine, essentially benevolent, view of Mother Nature derives from the fact that she performs her catastrophic feats of destruction -- volcanoes, earthquakes, tornadoes, hurricanes and floods -- in isolated episodes of limited scope and duration that, however tragic, soon fade from memory.

Ironically, her greatest acts of turmoil unfold so slowly that they often go practically undetected. Continents riding on the huge plates of the lithosphere, moving at a rate of a few centimeters per year, drift, collide, coalesce and re-fragment with profound consequences for living organisms.

The theory of plate tectonics offers a new interpretation of Mother Nature. In the modified, less anthropocentric version, she appears not as an actively concerned benefactor nor as a capricious, arbitrarily destructive force of violence but rather as a dispassionate combination of phenomena resulting from interactions of Earth's four great physical spheres -- the lithosphere, the hydrosphere, the atmosphere and the biosphere.

ICE AGE CATASTROPHE

Of all the catastrophes that befall our beleaguered biosphere, the great periods of glaciation, the ice ages, have proved the most devastating. Volcanic eruptions, earthquakes, and floods, however violent and destructive, cannot compare with the inexorable, all-encompassing force of an encroaching ice age.

The most recent cycle of ice began about 200 million years ago. Tectonic forces had pushed all the earth's land into one super-continent called Pangea, whose location near the equator permitted no glaciers. After a time, Pangea re-fragmented into numerous plates, the larger of which carry today's familiar continents. Some 65 million years ago, plates carrying the great land masses of Antarctica, Siberia, and North America began to drift into the polar regions.

As these great chunks of land moved closer to the poles, they began to radiate more heat into space than they gained from the sun during the day. Eventually the temperature cooled to the point where winter accumulations of snow near the north and south poles failed to melt during the summer. As more snow gathered, its cumulative weight compressed the lower layers into spreading sheets of ice. Thus began a long cooling trend, called the Cenozoic climate decline, that continues to this very day.

Fifteen million years ago, glaciers formed in Antarctica. Ten million years ago, small glaciers appeared on mountains in the higher latitudes of North America. Seven million years ago the great northern-hemisphere ice sheet began to grow and two and one-half million years ago a sheet of ice spread over Greenland. Vast accumulations of snow and ice reflected heat from the sun, accelerating Earth's downward spiral into the frigid embrace of the Pleistocene glaciation.

Since the advent of the Pleistocene Ice Age some two million years ago, Earth has endured at least four periods of extreme glaciation. During these four well documented events, walls of ice edged into Europe, devastating the countryside as far south as London and Moscow. Smaller glaciers spread northward from the Alps and Pyrenees, leaving only a narrow strip of tundra and scrubby pine forest between the two frozen landscapes. In North America, similar sheets of ice spread southward to the sites of modern-day Cincinnati and Philadelphia.

On each occasion comparable onslaughts of ice and snow pushed existing life forms, on land and in the sea, to the brink of extinction. Each time, the earth warmed, the ice retreated and life rebounded, multiplying in the warming seas and creeping back into the rubble left by the departing glaciers. Ironically, one species, destined to become the world's dominate animal, evolved against this backdrop of ice.

THE CLIMATE FORGE

Humans now live virtually everywhere on earth -- even spending extended periods of time under the ocean and in outer space. But once, according to anthropological consensus, our direct ancestors lived only in Africa.

Twenty-five million years ago, the African continent floated free, separated from Europe and Asia by the Tethys Sea. At that time, lush jungles, now found only in the Congo Basin, extended further north and east.

When Africa drifted into its present position, the bulk of the continent, that north of the equator, fell under the influence of the Atlantic sub-tropical anticyclone. The warm gently subsiding air from this permanent high-pressure system (called the Azores High) prevents upward vertical motion and cloud formation except in the very lowest two or three thousand feet.

The dry, sinking air from this high pressure cell has created the largest expanse of desert terrain in the world -- the Sahara/Arabian desert complex. This vast bleakness efficiently separates the verdant jungles and forests of equatorial Africa from the Mediterranean Sea and the fertile lands of Iran/Iraq. Even the Canary, Azores and Cape Verde islands, off Africa's west coast,

have arid climates except where mountains capture moisture from prevailing
ocean winds.

Thus, as the Pleistocene climate grew colder it also grew drier. In
equatorial Africa, home to our pre-human ancestors, large portions of the once
lush jungles and rain forests wilted and died from lack of rain. Lakes and
rivers dried up, grass and shrubs gradually replaced forests, and the desert
encroached from the north and south. Plants and animals, faced with
increasingly scarce sources of food and water, had to adapt to harsher
conditions, migrate equator ward with the changing environment -- or perish.

During this restive time, very human-like creatures foraged through the
mountains and valleys of Ethiopia. These versatile creatures, ancestral to all
Homo *sapiens*, adapted well to the chaotic changes. Forced out of the trees
onto the grassy savanna plains, they developed both physical and behavioral
flexibility that led ultimately to larger brains, bipedal locomotion and a refined
hand.

A million years later they had evolved into the first true humans, Homo
habilis -- so named because they used basic stone tools and built simple
shelters as they hunted, gathered and foraged over eastern Africa.

Habilis reigned for a half-million years, eventually disappearing in favor
of a more advanced species, Homo *erectus*. *Erectus*, an extremely successful
proto-human, survived for a million years, spreading throughout Africa and
migrating to Eurasia, China, Indonesia and Europe.

OUT OF AFRICA

Anthropologists have advanced fear, hunger, curiosity -- even a sense of
destiny -- as reasons for human migration out of Africa. More than likely,
however, early humans migrated simply because they needed to -- and
because they could.

Hunting, gathering and foraging requires a lot of individual turf.
Population increases generated competition for space in the more bountiful
hunting/gathering regions which forced nomadic groups to explore new
territories to the north and south. Ultimately, bands of Homo *erectus* found
themselves eking out a marginal existence along the fluctuating borders of the
Sahara desert. They could migrate no farther because, even assuming they

could carry some food and water, they would not survive long in that desolate wasteland.

For thousands of years *erectus* followed the greening desert fringes as they shifted northward during the summer monsoon rains and retreated in the fall when the rains ceased. Thus, *erectus* likely became the world's first weather observer and forecaster -- carefully watching for signs indicating the status of the monsoon.

About one million years ago the earth slipped into the first of the four great Pleistocene glaciations -- the Günz Ice Age. North Africa's climate responded with a dramatic change. The monsoon rains began to appear earlier in the season, they lasted longer and fell farther north than previously.

Slowly the desert retreated under the benevolent veil of an extended and prolonged rainy season. Grasses and bushes flourished where formerly nothing had existed but sand and rock. Rivers and wadies filled, and Lake Chad expanded to rival the Caspian Sea in size. Animals rushed to take advantage of the new profusion of plants, and humans followed.

Roving farther north, our *erectus* ancestors encountered seasonal weather for the first time. Summers became cooler and winters colder, with blustery storms sweeping in continually from the west. It became impractical, perhaps impossible, to retreat to the tropics during the low-sun seasons. But *erectus* knew how to use fire, make clothing and find or make shelter, and thus weathered the cyclic changes.

Eventually our *erectus* ancestors began watching the skies, attempting to foresee the coming weather. After a time, they recognized that, while certain clouds held no threat, others heralded an approaching storm and they should return home, or seek shelter and get a fire started. In time one tribal member, a person wiser and more observant than the others, acquired the chore of weather watching and warning -- and accumulating weather lore.

The world's early weather prognosticators no doubt suffered the same abuse as do modern forecasters. Imagine the indignities heaped upon him or her by the clan when, warned of an impending storm, called off the hunt, or abandoned a bountiful field of berries or grain, and hurried home in mid-day -- only to see the storm veer off and miss them entirely. Probably they made a joke (the world's first joke?) about the weather seer's incompetence.

"When Og say's it will rain, we should go forth and hunt and gather. When Og says it will not rain, we should stay in our cave close to the fire, make clothing and tools and draw on the cave walls."

One day a million or more years ago, a small band working their way through a forest of Aleppo pine looked up to see an immense body of water. They had discovered the Mediterranean Sea. The fortuitous change in global climate had temporarily created large green corridors through the Sahara desert over which early Homo *erectus* could hunt and gather -- and migrate out of Africa to new worlds.

Warm periods, much like the one in which we currently dwell, intervened between each Ice Age. The glaciers retreated and desert conditions returned to North Africa, closing the climate gate to the mid-east and ending, for a time at least, migration into and out of Equatorial Africa. Plants, animals and humans, caught in the resurgent deserts, worked their way back to the tropics or northward to the Mediterranean Sea. Humans remaining in the north migrated eastward along the Mediterranean into the Mideast and thence to Eurasia, Asia and Europe. Isolated from their southern cousins by the vast Sahara desert, the northern branches of the human race continued to evolve but in slightly different ways depending upon the environments they encountered.

THE WÜRM ICE AGE

Homo *sapiens,* modern, the third and latest version of our human species, appeared in Africa about 100 thousand years ago, just as the earth began its slide into the coldest portion of the Pleistocene -- the Würm glacial era.

About 60 thousand years ago, fully modern humans living in the region now known as the Sahara Desert, developed a refined tool-making technique called the "Aterian" (first discovered at el Ater in eastern Algeria). The Arterians left samples of their unique stone tools across the continent from the Atlantic Ocean almost to the Nile River, and into the desert as far south as Niger and Chad. They also left rock sculptures and cave paintings rivaling, and antedating, those of the famed Lascaux caves in France. These practical and artistic artifacts reveal a climate that supported hunting, animal husbandry and local cultivation of cereals some 40 to 60 thousand years ago -- a time that coincides with the most recent (and one of coldest) glacial periods of the Pleistocene -- the Würm Ice Age.

Habitation of North Africa during the Würm suggests that wetter, more hospitable climates occurred in the Sahara during previous Ice Ages as well --

either at the peak of glaciation or during one of the transitional phases into or out of glaciation.

During the Würm glacial era, Earth's temperature dropped some 10 degrees overall, and the polar ice caps grew to immense size. At the peak of glaciation, continuous sheets of ice extended beyond the Great Lakes in North America and covered Europe as far south as England and Denmark while ice bergs and broken ice floes filled the North Atlantic between Newfoundland and England. In the southern hemisphere, the Antarctic ice sheet reached outward an additional 100 miles. At times it bridged the Drake Passage and joined the glaciers pushing out of the southern Andes onto the Patagonia Plains.

Intense cooling by the glaciers in eastern North American and western Europe anchored deep troughs of cold air in those regions while the relatively warm oceanic waters maintained a weak ridge of high pressure over the North Atlantic. In North America, nothing but a narrow strip of tundra and alpine forest separated frigid glacial air from warm tropical air residing over the Gulf of Mexico. Continual surges of Arctic air flowed directly from the glacier into the gulf with little or no modification.

The explosive mixture of cold, dry air and warm, moist air generated a steady series of storms in The Gulf of Mexico. Guided by the strong prevailing westerlies, they crossed the Atlantic well south of today's storm tracks, quickly reaching Spain or North Africa.

Geodetic parameters (the earth's dimensions, rotation and gravity) physically limit the position of subtropical anticyclonic circulation to regions between 40° north and south of the equator. The centers of the subtropical highs, however, move seasonally about five or six degrees of latitude -- pole ward in summer and equator ward in winter.

During an ice age, especially an ice-age winter, westerly winds would flow much stronger and much closer to the equator than nowadays. Under these conditions, the intensity of the Atlantic anticyclone decreased and shifted slightly southward, losing much of its desiccating effect on North Africa. As a result, storm clouds grew to greater heights and carried significant amounts of moisture into the West Africa interior. Rivers and lakes filled and, with each passing storm, vegetation extended farther inland through northern Mauritania, northern Mali and western Algeria.

In Europe, a slightly different situation existed. The Alps, the Pyrenees and the Massif Central in France form a barrier between cold, European continental air and the relatively warm, moist air over the Mediterranean Sea. The Carcassonne Gap and the Rhone River Valley, however, breech this mountain chain. During Ice Ages, as during current winter seasons, air pouring into the Gulf of Leon through these openings made the western Mediterranean, then even more than now, an area of intense cyclone development (cyclogenesis).

Again, with the desiccating effects of the Atlantic High diminished, clouds and moisture within the storm systems reached greater heights. A steady series of cold fronts from the Mediterranean pushed into northern Africa, spreading rainfall deep into the deserts of Algeria, Libya and Egypt.

In the southern hemisphere, the "roaring forties" became the roaring thirties. Strong westerly winds flowing across the Andes in South America maintained an upper-air trough east of Rio de Janeiro, with a wedge of high pressure in the South Atlantic.

The South Atlantic subtropical high-pressure cell underwent a reduction in intensity similar to its North Atlantic counterpart. It shifted slightly north and east where it continued to provide a strong flow of moist tropical air across the equator into western North Africa. Reduced subsidence from the North Atlantic High permitted monsoon moisture flowing into North Africa to reach greater heights, allowing greater quantities of rain to fall throughout Mauritania, Mali, Niger and Chad.

With the drying effect of the North Atlantic Anticyclone reduced, rainfall -- and consequently vegetation -- increased throughout North Africa. Cooler, ice-age temperatures reduced the rate of evaporation and enhanced the effects of the increased rainfall. Moisture accumulated in the soil, moderating the surface temperature and providing an additional source of moisture for storms arriving from the west and north.

The Würm glaciation alternated between relatively cold and warm periods. Recent cores taken from the Greenland ice sheet indicate six or seven episodes of glacial advance and retreat over the last 100 thousand years. Paleoclimatologists now reason that similar fluctuations occurred also during other Ice Ages.

Without more accurate timing of northern hemisphere glacial periods and pluvial events in North Africa, exact correlation between the two remains speculative. Still, archaeological discoveries make it obvious that Homo *sapiens* occupied many regions of the Sahara desert at some time during the Würm glacial period. It seems at least possible that Homo *erectus* also migrated northward from equatorial Africa to the Mediterranean Sea and beyond during earlier glacial episodes.

Ironically, the fantastically destructive Pleistocene Ice Ages may have provided the motivating force that propelled humankind to its remarkably successful development and habitation of this vast and essentially hostile planet.

APPENDIX A

SUB-TROPICAL ANTICYCLONES
HOW THEY WORK

Earth's tropical belt, between 30°N and 30°S, gains more heat from the sun each day than it loses by radiation into space. The excess heat, conveyed upward in rising air thermals, spreads northward and southward. When air moves poleward into the mid-latitudes, a strange force, called the Coriolis Force, steers it to the right. By the time it reaches about 30 to 40 degrees north latitude, the air streaming out of the tropics has acquired a nearly west to east direction.

As the tropical air turns eastward, an over-abundance accumulates in the upper atmosphere forming the high pressure cells that dominate subtropical latitudes in both hemispheres. Some of this excess air moves laterally north. Most gradually moves southward and sinks back to the earth's surface forming the warm, dry subtropical anticyclone belt. A similar sequence occurs in the southern hemisphere.

High pressure at the center of a subtropical anticyclone forces air outward around its perimeter. The Coriolis Force gently steers this outward flowing air into a clockwise (anticyclonic) circulation in the northern hemisphere and counter-clockwise (anticyclonic) motion in the southern hemisphere. Air flowing gently toward the equator from the equatorial portions of the subtropical anticyclones in both hemispheres, called the "Trade Winds" by early wind-jamming sailors, converge near the equator. The converging winds force air upward, enhancing the normal rising motions of tropical air and concentrating them into a narrow band of intense convective thunderstorms which mark the Inter-Tropical Convergence Zone (ITCZ).

Meteorologists call such a large, more or less closed, meridional circulation of rising and sinking tropical air a Hadley Cell circulation, named after George Hadley who first discovered the phenomena in the 18th century.

The warm, dry subsiding air in the eastern sides of Hadley Cell circulations suppresses cloud formation and contributes greatly to the development and maintenance of deserts in equatorial regions of both hemispheres around the world.

CHAPTER FOUR

THE PRE-DAWN OF CIVILIZATION

Wherein we follow the adventures of early humans as they migrated out of Africa and into Eurasia where for a million years they suffered, endured and survived erratic changes in climate that molded their abilities to not only adapt and prevail but to continue to evolve, developing social skills that permitted them to exploit natural resources and ultimately develop agriculture and civilization.

"The first form of culture is agriculture. It is when man settles down to till the soil and lay up provisions for the uncertain future that he finds time and reason to be civilized."
-- Will Durant

TO ADAPT AND SURVIVE

Human life originated in the warm climate of equatorial Africa where bountiful supplies of food existed. Inevitably, however, competition for living space created pressure that forced the weakest groups to move on, frequently into less abundant lands. Some groups eventually found themselves eking out a meager existence hunting and gathering along the southern fringes of the Sahara desert.

On occasion, fortuitous changes in African climate caused rain to fall over the desert. Green corridors appeared over which adventuresome tribes crossed the Sahara to the shores of the Mediterranean. As they foraged along the Mediterranean shores, across the Nile Delta and into the "Fertile Crescent" of the Near East, they encountered only the best of conditions. Ample vegetation supported plentiful game and migrating groups supplemented their diet with roots, nuts and fruits.

Still, competition for favorable sites forced the less able to move on, leaving the most fit to hold the more amicable areas. Always the pressure came from the more congenial lands and always it ended with people along the margins forced outward to live on increasingly cold and arid lands that could barely support them.

The forced migration continued eastward into the Mid-east, India and Asia, and into southern Europe along the Mediterranean Sea where humans necessarily learned to adapt to changing circumstances and new environments. As yet, however, they had not gained the necessary skills to survive the rigorous ice-age climates that frequented territories north of the great glacier-covered mountain chain weaving through southern Europe and Asia.

The two most recent glacial episodes, the Riss and the Würm, featured intense cold periods interrupted periodically by warm, interstadial, periods. A very warm period -- the Eemian interglacial era, with a climate comparable to or even warmer than the Holocene interglacial that we currently enjoy -- occurred between the Riss and the Würm glaciations.

During the Eemian, as with our present interglacial period, the ice sheets retreated and prevailing storm tracks moved far north of their Ice Age position. The desiccating effects of the Atlantic sub-tropical high, suppressed during the glacial periods, increased and the sub-tropical regions of North Africa, the Mideast, and western Asia. became much warmer and drier. Grass and shrubs replaced wilted forests as the land reverted to semi-arid steppe and patches of barren desert.

North of the great ice-capped Eurasian mountain chain, rain began to fall instead of snow. The earth flowered as the permafrost melted and plants quickly sprang to life in the ruined landscape left by the retreating glaciers. The almost treeless zone of tundra and taioga fronting the ice-sheets moved far to the north, replaced by vast expanses of grass. The great herds of horse, mammoth, reindeer, bison and other animals, well adapted to ice-age cold, followed the retreating tundra northward. Farther south, forests of broad-leaved trees as well as animals from the more temperate southern regions surged onto the plains of the Eurasian steppe.

During the Eemian, humans who could control fire and construct suitable clothing and shelter to ward off the winter cold began to move progressively farther north where they found a bounty of fish, game and edible plants.

Some continued north and remained primarily hunters and gatherers, following the immense migrating herds. Others found themselves living on the drier, grassy steppe lands where they maintained semi-permanent camps from which they ventured to forage. Still others remained further south, near the mountains with their forests and rivers, and adopted a nomadic gatherer/hunter/fisher life style, drifting north and south with the seasons.

When the glaciers returned, they all crowded southward competing for increasingly fewer resources. Many perished in the flight from the encroaching ice sheets. Some holed up in mountain caves and some returned to the warmer lands south of the mountains where they encountered additional competition from new human immigrants arriving from Africa.

For a million years humans suffered, endured and survived periods of environmental disruption wrought by such eccentric changes in climate. Even during the coldest and warmest periods, large, rapid and seeming random fluctuations in temperature challenged Man's abilities to adapt and prevail.

But they did survive. Archeologists have uncovered remains of ancestral humans (generally *erectus* but possibly some *habilis* as well) who lived in Indonesia, China, India, Eurasia and Europe at least one million years ago. Judging from this limited but widespread fossil evidence, hominids, exposed to repeated shifts in climate and habitat, developed large brains which, combined with increased manual dexterity, enabled them to accommodate a wide variety of environmental hazards and setbacks.

ICE AGE LIVING

During ice ages, winter ruled the land. Even on the hottest days of summer, thoughts rarely strayed from the need to stockpile food and fuel and construct shelter for the long, cold winter that would soon arrive.

Most of the winter snow fell and accumulated on the ice, nourishing the glacier and leaving the land to the south dry and frozen. Shallow masses of frigid air, cooled by contact with the glacial surface, flowed down the ice sheet and burst onto the steppes with a speed that sometimes exceeded one hundred miles per hour. The howling winds, varying in intensity but never stopping, whipped the scant snowfall across the bleak frozen land and picked up clouds of pulverized rock that glaciers had ground to a floury texture.

Human shelters, little more than loosely woven branches constructed over a shallow pit and plastered with mud or covered with skins, provided little comfort. They did, however, furnish a slight protection from the constant wind and a place for fire where burning bones or half-wet logs provided essential warmth.

In spring, the meager winter snow melted as did the permafrost. Shallow rooted grasses and herbs sprouted and grew rapidly on the windswept plains. By mid-summer, a great variety of animals grazed the rich grasslands providing essential food, fuel and clothing for glacial steppe dwellers.

THE ADVENT OF MODERN MAN

While occupying much of the habitable portions of Africa, Eurasia, Asia and Europe for hundreds of thousands of years, our pre-*sapiens* ancestors remained essentially a passive component of the natural order of life. They adapted to whatever life styles the environment afforded them. They hunted and collected wild foods and drifted, whenever possible, with their accustomed climate.

The continuous use of one primitive (acheulean) type of hand ax for over a million years illustrates the painfully slow rate of technological progress in the early stages of human development. Not until the advent of Homo *sapiens*, modern, gifted and dynamic humans, with their more innovative brains, did there occur any significant changes in tool making, shelter building or hunting techniques. Even Neanderthals, once considered an intermediate *sapiens*, employed only rudimentary tools.

Archeologists have unearthed evidence that modern humans began using more advanced technological processes about 120 thousand years ago. Some 50,000 years ago, during the Würm glaciation, they began to migrate out of Africa into the mid-east and points north and east.

Homo *sapiens* spread rapidly across the earth, appearing in Eurasia and Europe between 40,000 and 35,000 years ago. By about 25,000 years ago, *H. sapiens* had replaced all older forms of human life.

NEANDERTHAL -- THE PENULTIMATE HUMAN

Neanderthal Man, possibly a descendant of Homo *erectus*, appeared mysteriously about 200 thousand years ago, lived primarily in Europe, and disappeared about 30 thousand years ago. Neanderthal's nearly 200 thousand year tenure on Earth stretched over two of the coldest periods of the Pleistocene -- The Riss (180 to 130 thousand years ago) and the Würm (80 to 10 thousand years ago) Ice Ages.

Under the Eemian interglacial, between 130 and 80 thousand years ago, a benign climate prevailed -- one quite similar to that which now exists. As the glaciers retreated, life surged once again onto the Eurasian steppes. During this 50,000 year respite from ice and snow, Neanderthal Man spread rapidly north as well as east and west. But, although they possessed language, aesthetic sensibility, artistic talent, weapons, tools and the control of fire, they had not yet developed the capability to do much more than partake of the natural abundance that unfolded as they advanced into new territories.

Eventually they roamed as far north as England and as far east as Uzbekistan in Russia. When the glaciers returned, they retreated southward and, about 30 thousand years ago, they disappeared from Europe -- although a few clans may have survived longer in the Near East.

Creatures depending on special characteristics for survival, unable to quickly change habitat or diet, often perished during major changes in environment. Neanderthal man, stocky, tough and well suited for an ice-age environment, survived quite well until Modern Man arrived. Then he disappeared.

The demise of Neanderthal Man coincides suspiciously with the arrival of modern Homo *sapiens* (the wise one, also known as Cro-Magnon Man and, sometimes, Advanced Hunter) who invaded Europe 40 thousand years ago. The two peoples apparently coexisted for a time -- perhaps until about 25,000 years ago in the Near East -- but some ten thousand years after Cro-Magnon arrived in Europe, the Neanderthals and their culture had faded and vanished.

THE EXPLOSION

H. sapiens arrived from the east, appearing first in central Europe and then in western Europe. His arrival 40 thousand years ago marked the beginning of the Upper Paleolithic era. By 35 thousand years ago, they had replaced all previous versions of humans and occupied Europe and Asia as far north as England, and as far east as Lake Biakal and Beijing bringing with them their greatly advanced skills in hunting, tool making, language and art.

Anatomically modern, with large and clever brains, they survived the long, harsh Würm glaciation by applying novel solutions to constantly changing conditions. With their sophisticated social skills, they exploited all available natural resources to develop improved shelter and clothing. They used their advanced hunting techniques to hunt the great herds of bison, reindeer, horse and mammoth that abounded on the open steppe and tundra of Europe and stockpiled food for an uncertain future.

Paradoxically, this coldest period of the Pleistocene ice age seemed to spark a blossoming of social and economic complexities as well as improved technology and art. The decorative artifacts left by these ice-age dwellers indicate an evolution of social status and hierarchy and the emergence of a symbolic plane of beliefs and values.

ON THE BRINK OF CIVILIZATION

By 26 thousand years ago, their complex cultural advancements included the establishment of larger more or less permanent communities where they fashioned a variety of highly refined weapons and tools made from bone and antler as well as stone. They stored food for winter and traded goods over long distances. They carved animal figurines, produced ivory beads, pendants and other body ornaments and painted glorious murals on their caves.

Conditions changed radically as the ice began to melt around 18 thousand years ago. Floods from melting glaciers and the invasion of open pastures by forests forced big changes on the Neolithic European people. Some followed the great herds of reindeer and other foraging animals as they moved northward while others remained, shifting their dependence from big game to smaller animals and supplementing their diet with fish, fowl and wild vegetable foods.

As the climate mellowed, people accumulated into ever larger communities. They refined decision-making hierarchies to regulate social relations and behavior; established trade routes along the rivers; practiced some tillage and husbandry; hunted fished and gathering shellfish.

CLIMATE, SOIL AND CIVILIZATION

When the Würm Ice Age ended about 12 thousand years ago, an energetic, adventuresome, innovative people stood prepared to embrace the ensuing warmth of the Holocene, abandon the uncertain life of hunter-gatherer and adopt a more secure life of agriculture -- leading, ultimately, to civilization.

At first glance, the region composed of Asia Minor, the Near East and Middle East seems a highly unlikely region for Man to make the singularly important leap to systematic agriculture. The entire area lies under the desiccating influence of dry continental air flowing from interior Eurasia. The gentle downward anticyclonic motion of this air suppresses cloud development, and therefore rainfall, maintaining a desert or semi-desert climate throughout Syria, Lebanon, Israel and Jordan -- the lands comprising the region called the Levant.

In winter invading storms from the Mediterranean Sea interrupt the flow of air from the Eurasian continent to bring marginal rainfall to the area, most of which falls in the higher mountain terrain. During summers -- April or early May through September or early October -- practically no rain falls and little vegetation grows without irrigation. Only a narrow band -- the Fertile Crescent -- extending along the Mediterranean coastline from Israel to the Anatolian rise and thence eastward and southeastward along the foothills of the Zagros mountains in southwestern Iran, collects sufficient rainfall to grow crops without supplemental irrigation.

Fifteen thousand years ago, a significantly different climate prevailed in the Levant. The permanent high-pressure cell positioned over the Eurasian ice sheet forced mid-latitude cyclones to move on a more southerly track than today. Even in summer, storms would develop in the eastern Mediterranean Sea and move into the Near East, making the climate cooler and rainier than now. Some rain fell in summertime and significant rain fell during the winter, producing a relatively verdant land with an abundance of plants and animals.

THE FIRST FARMERS

No one knows who planted the first crops or domesticated the first animals. Incipient farming practices may have developed several times in different places over the millennia. But anthropologists generally credit the Natufians for the first extensive and systematic exploitation of natural resources --

including farming and domestication of animals. It appears that an opportune juxtaposition of ability and natural resources occurred in the Near East which gave rise to agriculture and, ultimately, civilization.

Fifteen thousand years ago, the Levant, a lush hill country now occupied by Israel, Syria, Lebanon and Jordan, boasted a profusion of plants and animals. One group of hunter-gathers who lived in the Levant, the Natufians, had already established a high level of social organization and used a variety of methods to exploit available resources. But, as the Würm Ice Age waned, the world warmed and the region experienced repeated droughts. Hemmed in by the mountains to the north and spreading deserts to the south and east, they adopted an increasing reliance on domesticated food.

Their fortuitous location, offering a blending of fertile soil and a warm climate, eased their transition to an agrarian style of life. For here, between the Nile delta and Persia, both the wild grasses ancestral to our cereals and wild animals ancestral to our modern sheep, goats and cattle evolved.

The relatively mellow climate of the eastern Mediterranean region favored fast-growing plants. In winter, cool moist air from the Mediterranean stimulated early growth. Grains could grow, mature, and seed themselves before the parching summer winds arrived from Eurasia and Arabia. Soon rippling fields of wheat and barley materialized and flourished.

Humans, anxious to glean this abundance of easily attainable food, had to work quickly because ears of wild grain shatter as soon as the plants reach maturity. Sometimes, if the summer is hotter than usual, a mature field of grain can turn to a field of barren stalks in as little as a week. As they trekked north and south, foraging for food, humans probably kept a watch on the seasons and returned repeatedly to particularly bountiful fields.

In time, the more clever tribes saw the advantage in remaining close to such fields and, about 12 thousand years ago, began to build permanent settlements that featured elaborate stone houses with paved areas for food preparation and storage for the wild grains that proliferated nearby.

James Michener, in his book, *"The Source,"* offers a vivid portrayal of a small group of pre-historic humans balanced delicately on the edge of civilization some 10 thousand years ago on a spot destined to become the land of Galilee.

In Michener's story, Ur, his wife and an extended family of six other groups eked out a hunter-gather existence, as did the occupants of this land for 200 thousand years previously. In a climate becoming precariously more dry with time, they hunted lion and boar and gathered wild cereal grains which they ground into flour and stored for the winter.

Ur's wife and her flint-knapper son built the clan's first permanent dwelling so she could more closely watch the grain fields she had cultivated from the wild grains that grew haphazardly in the area. Her son invented the flint sickle for harvesting the grain efficiently.

As the crops grew in importance so grew their fear of a harvest failure. The cultivated grains, which freed them from the unpredictable fortunes of the hunt, tied them to the land and thus subjected them to the vicissitudes of the weather and climate. Ur's wife knew that these forces of nature had a living spirit. How else to explain the flash of lightning that tore a tree in half and set fire to forests, or the unexpected cloudburst that washed away their fields?

When storms threatened the wheat with fire and flood, or drought and desiccating winds burned the wheat as it stood in the fields, she realized that the crops had become too valuable to trust the harvest to chance. One day, when lightning started a fire that wiped out half the grain crop, she concluded that their complacency and abundance had offended the spirits. Accordingly she erected a monolith to the spirits of the wind and the rain. Thus they illustrated their recognition of the spirits power and symbolized their desire to offend no longer.

One day, Ur's wife, standing in her grain field, watched Ur and his fellow hunters return from the hunt dragging a boar. As she saw them outlined against the ripening wheat, she glimpsed a future in which men would no longer dash off to the hunt but would remain closer to home and tend the grain.

Who can say it didn't happen just so?

CLIMATE SETBACK

Bands of semi-nomadic people gathered and hunted the plants and animals that thrived in the verdant hills and valleys of the Near East. As the earth warmed and the ice age waned, however, Mediterranean storms decreased in number and intensity and the Levant experienced increasingly frequent droughts. Gradually it reverted to arid or semi-arid desert. Of necessity, they began to cultivate the progressively dwindling fields of wild grain and eventually to domesticate animals.

It seems at least possible that agriculture and pastoralism developed independently in several widely separated places. Primitive communities of hunters and food-gatherers would naturally adopt the form of agriculture most suited to the existing climate and the soil upon which they found themselves. Any grass soil, populated by people at a certain stage of mental growth, and under certain climatic constraints, might give rise to pastoralism. Similarly, alluvial soils such as existed in the great river valleys, populated by equally intelligent peoples and under similar climatic constraints, might tend to produce the beginnings of tillage.

In Anatolia and the Levant, large agricultural communities cultivated plots of wheat and barley before they domesticated animals. They remained largely dependent on hunting for their meat until the late eighth millennium. During the same period, quasi-nomadic tribes in the nearby Zagros mountains domesticated sheep and goats but practiced only limited tillage. Hunting and plant gathering continued to provide a substantial part of their diet.

CIVILIZATION

Thus, the amicable warming of the Holocene provided the means as well as the milieu and impetus for the human rise to civilization. Many substantial towns sprang up in the early centers of mixed farming. The discovery of irrigation greatly increased the size of cultivated fields. In turn, greater food production permitted larger populations and the development of advanced urban civilizations -- and attendant advances in social organization.

The great early civilizations did not originate in the uplands where easily exhausted soils forced a semi-nomadic life. Rather, Man, possibly urged by an increasingly dry climate, built the first cities and developed the first civilizations along the rivers where dependable sources of water existed and annual floods continually renewed the soil with a fresh layer of fertile silt. The four primal Eurasian civilizations arose in semi-arid lands and grew dependent upon the alluvial soils of the Nile, the Euphrates-Tigris, the Indus and the Whang-Ho river systems.

Sumer led the way in the development of cities -- although rivaling Egypt soon followed with her unique version of civilization. The Sumerians developed and produced a wide variety of new devices and techniques, including metals, wheels, boats and -- most important -- writing. But the contention of great powers in the Near East and Mediterranean, led by ambitious kings with well-equipped armies, unfortunately led to a depletion of resources and the eventual decline of the ancient civilizations in Mesopotamia and Egypt. The migration of new centers of growth -- and of new human outlooks -- shifted to the west.

CHAPTER FIVE

THE GREEK EXPERIENCE

Wherein we glimpse a new order of civilization. While other cultures submitted and suffered in a world diverging ever farther from reality, the Greeks embraced an energetic enthusiasm for life and nourished a new, quite different, perspective -- a supremacy of mind in the affairs of men that led to speculations on the meaning of life and the nature of the earth and efforts to provide physical explanations for natural phenomena. Through the power of pure reasoning, they advanced the physical understanding of medicine, mathematics, astronomy, physics and meteorology far beyond previous experience.

"That which distinguishes the modern world from the ancient, and that which divides the West from the East, is the supremacy of mind in the affairs of men, and this came to birth in Greece and lived in Greece alone of all the ancient world."

-- Edith Hamilton

CLIMATE, GEOGRAPHY AND PHILOSOPHY

As the Holocene dawned, between 12 and 9 thousand years ago, people began to cultivate suitable species of cereal grains and root crops in a few places in each of the major land masses. Scenes of early agriculture appeared in Southwest Asia, equatorial Africa, the Southeast Asian mainland, Central

America, and lowland and highland South America. At the same time Man began to domesticate livestock, at first for food and later to pull wagons or plows or to carry loads. Within a few thousand years of its origin, agriculture had spread nearly to its modern geophysical limits.

Systematic farming apparently originated in the Levant where a fortuitous combination of climate and human resources prevailed. But a climate similar to that of the Levant exists throughout the Mediterranean region and the art of farming spread rapidly from the first settlements of the lower Sumerian plains into Europe. By 6500 BC, farmer pioneers had entered Europe at the Bosporous (Instanbul) and established hamlets in Macedonia and Thessalonia on the Greek peninsula. As early as 5000 BC, the practice of cultivating crops and domesticating animals had spread to Greece, Crete, Italy, southern France and Spain.

As the droughty Levant seems an unlikely place for humans to develop agriculture, so does the harsh, mountainous region of Greece seem an unlikely place for the intellectual revolution of mind and spirit that occurred there.

The high north to south chain of the Pindhos divides Northern Greece. Subsidiary ranges to the west continue to the sea, leaving few cultivable plains and fewer harbors. East of the divide, east-to-west transverse ranges divide the Thessalian plain from Macedon, Boeotia from Thessaly, and Attica from Boeotia. In the south, only the narrow Isthmus of Corinth connects the jagged Peloponnisos from the mainland.

The sun rises high over this craggy land, and shines abundantly during summers. In July and August the prevailing dry northerly wind (the "Etesian" wind of the ancients) dominates, maintaining clear skies and dry, relatively cool weather.

Serious rains customarily begin in October with a maximum in December. Although winter arrives in December and lasts through April, the warm Mediterranean and Aegean seas surrounding the Greek peninsula moderate the cold. Snow, if it falls, seldom lies long on the plain of Attica. In April and May, rising temperatures bring a sudden rush of flowers and grass. In the lowlands, crops ripen before the end of May.

The pleasant Greek climate belies the difficulty of its terrain. Unlike the alluvial valleys of the Ganges, the Indus, the Tigris, the Euphrates or the Nile, Grecian soil lies thin over a rocky substrata. Fruit and vegetables grow only in a few fertile plains or in terraces and holes carved in hillsides and held by stone embankments. The land cannot maintain flocks or herds on any large scale. Olive oil takes the place of butter.

THE ROAD TO PHILOSOPHY

Climate and geography play a significant role in determining the character and philosophy of a people. Historians have suggested that the rugged terrain and sparse fertility of the Greek peninsula influenced and shaped the character and destiny of its people and contributed to the Greeks unique approach to the world and life. Hippocrates himself suggested that only in such lands as Greece, "bare, waterless, rough, oppressed by winter's storms and burnt by the sun," could produce "hard, lean, vigilant, energetic, independent, well-articulated, well-braced and hairy" men.

The world in which the Greek experience emerged -- and ultimately dominated -- occurred at a time when reason played only the smallest role in daily life. All contemporary, Egyptian and Asiatic, civilizations featured wretched, subjugated peoples ruled by enthroned despots. Equally well established priestly organizations directed all intellectual forces toward the spiritual world rather than the physical one. All-important things belonged to the domain of the unseen inner spirit while facts and reality, everything that made up the visible, sensible, audible world, played only an indirect part.

While Egypt and Asia submitted and suffered in a world diverging ever farther from reality, the Greeks embraced an energetic enthusiasm for life and nourished a quite different perspective. For the first time, in Greece, thought became secular.

Rather than submit to dogmatic assertion and attribute all acts of nature to the inexplicable whims of the gods, early Greek philosophers searched for the ruling principles underlying the forces of nature. Their unique concept of the world, and their common-sense approach to investigation, initiated a transition from superstition and myth to science and philosophy. Although they lacked the means of modern scientific approach, their speculations on the meaning of life and the nature of the earth led them to precocious insights into weather phenomena and theories surprisingly close to such modern concepts as atoms and sub-atomic particles.

MINOAN PHILOSOPHERS

The ultimate Greek nation began as two main factions. Over the centuries relatively primitive Ionian and Aeolian herder/farmer tribes gradually infiltrated from the north (sometimes peacefully, sometimes not) and brought the Greek language with them. At about the same time, traders from Asia minor established several centers of culture in and around the Aegean Sea. The Mycenians in Peloponnesia achieved a relatively advanced degree of culture by 1500 BC including colonies on the west coast of Turkey. The Minoan culture prospered on Crete as early as 3000 BC reaching its apogee in the 16th century BC.

Around 1200 BC, the Dorians arrived from the north. In short time they conquered Peloponnesia, almost completely destroying the Mycenaean society, and soon after occupied Crete and the remaining island cultures. These events left Greece in a state of chaos and turmoil from which it would take centuries to recover. The prosperous trade with the west dwindled, war flourished and Greek culture languished.

Although the Dorian invasions submerged the old Aegean culture and plunged mainland Greece into a state of comparative barbarism, the Greek Ionian colonies remained relatively unscathed. The Ionians preserved the former Aegean culture and became, for a time, the world's most progressive civilization.

Along that narrow strip of Anatolian coast where, according to Herodotus, "the air and climate are the most beautiful in the whole world," the Ionians built twelve cities from which they conducted a fabulously successful international trade. Miletus, the southernmost of the twelve, became the richest city in the Greek world. Wealth created leisure which encouraged the growth of culture and, in this stimulating environment, Greece developed its two most illustrious endowments to the world -- science and philosophy.

METEOROLOGY AND MYTH

The earliest Greek philosophers made no clear distinction between questions of philosophy, science, and religion, or between scientific methods and magical procedures, or even between history and myth. They, as did the Sumerians and Egyptians, associated all natural phenomena, especially weather, with the activities of semi-anthropomorthic deities.

Aeolis raised gales blowing on his conch shell while Zeus cleaved the sky with bolts of lightning, followed by thunder and the many-hued rainbow of Iris.

Eos, the Greek goddess of the dawn, gave birth to the four cardinal winds, Boreas (the north wind), Zephyrus (the west wind of spring), Eurus (the east wind) and Notus (the south wind).

Zeus, supreme ruler of the gods, Lord of the Sky, the Rain-god, god of the storm-cloud who wielded the terrible thunderbolt, appointed Aeolus as his "keeper of the winds." Aeolus kept all the adverse winds tied in a leather bag but, unfortunately, placed the bag in the care of Odysseus. Odysseus' companions opened the bag out of curiosity and released the malicious winds onto the world -- with subsequent dire consequences.

The legend of Demeter neatly explains the seasons.

Zeus lived in the heavens as did most of the gods. But two very important deities, Demeter, The Goddess of Corn who brought forth the grain, and Dionysus, the God of the vine, dwelled and ruled supreme on earth.

Because they lived on the earth, these two divinities, the happy gods of food and drink, knew pain as well as joy. For after the harvest the black frost appeared, killing the fresh green life of the fields. As winter settled over the land, Demeter and Dionysus knew sorrow.

It was not always thus.

In one of the more catastrophic misdeeds of the generally incalculable gods, Hades, the lord of the dark underworld, abducted Demeter's only daughter and carried her away to the depths of the earth. Demeter, in her terrible grief, withheld her gifts from the earth. That year, a year of dreadfully severe suffering for all people, the green and flowering land became icebound and lifeless as winter overtook the earth. Nothing grew and it seemed the whole of mankind would die of famine.

At last Zeus realized he must take the matter in hand. He sent a number of gods to reason with Demeter but she would not hear them. Never again would she let the earth bear fruit until she had seen her daughter. Finally Zeus dispatched Hermes to bid Hades to release Persephone.

Hades knew that he must obey Zeus and agreed to let Persephone go but only after he tricked her into eating a pomegranate seed -- knowing that if she ate it she must return to him. Zeus then sent his mother, Rhea, to Demeter to negotiate a settlement.

Hades drove a hard bargain. In the end, Demeter agreed to send her lovely young daughter, Persephone, the maiden of spring and summer, into the dark world of the dead for four months each year. During Persephone's absence, desolation falls upon the barren, leafless earth. When Persephone once more steps upon the dry, brown landscape, fruits, flowers and leaves bloom again on the earth and all mankind joins Demeter in joyous celebration. That's why we have winter. Thank Zeus we also have spring.

If it seemed natural to associate thunder, storms, earthquakes and the growth of crops to the activity of some divine agency, so did it seem reasonable to attribute inspiring thought, qualms of conscience or onslaughts of passion to them as well. If the rain comes from Zeus, why should not a happy thought come from Athene. But, while the Greeks frequently attributed unusual events to acts of whimsical or willful gods, a few also questioned the ultimate nature of the world.

GREEK SCIENCE

The Greek philosophers attempted to provide physical explanations for natural phenomena and to explain the complexity of the world by reducing it to the interplay of primary constituents. In so doing they laid the foundations of modern science.

Thales, generally considered the founder of Greek science, and his contemporaries, Anaximander and Anaximenes, lived in the Ionian city of Miletus during the seventh and sixth centuries B.C. All came to the conclusion that some single physical entity or element formed the foundation of all material things in the world. Their thoughts differed mainly in the selection of the basic element. At the time, Greeks philosophers recognized only four terrestrial elements -- earth, air, water or fire.

Thales selected water as the primary substance. His choice missed the mark widely, as did those of all the early philosophers. The proposal itself, however, initiated a new approach to viewing and understanding the world without invoking gods or demons.

Anaximander decided that the earth and heavens arose from some eternal and ageless substance other than the ordinary elements. He decided that earthly matter was not constructed from any particular kind of material, such as water or earth, but some pervasive, imperishable and eternal substance he called *apeiron*.

Anaximenes, a generation later, took a slightly different approach. He noticed that clouds materialized from air and that rain fell from the clouds. He concluded, therefore, that all things derive from air through a complex processes of condensation and rarefaction. When rarefied, air became warmer and so tended to fire. When condensed, it grew colder and tended towards the solid.

Xenophanes, a contemporary of Anaximenes, thought earth might be the fundamental element. He found seashells in the mountains and assumed (correctly) that the physical characteristics of the earth changed with time. He also assumed (correctly) that the mountains at one time lay under the sea and had risen from the sea to their present height.

Still later, Heraclitus looked at fire, which emanates from the earth's bowels bringing new rocks to the earth while burning trees and other materials transformed into air. Accordingly, he decided that fire, ever-changing and capable of bringing change in other things, must be the elementary substance of the universe.

Anaxagoras, in the fifth century, revived Anaximander's concept of apeiron and carried it a step further. He envisioned a force, which he called Nous or Mind. This force interacted with an infinite number of small, invisible and indestructible, atom-like, particles and produced the material that composes the earth and the heavens.

Parmenides and later, Empedocles, held the belief that matter does not change. Where Thales selected water, Anaximenes air, Heraclitus fire and Xenophanes earth as the primary element, Paramenides and Empedocles believed that objects emerge through various minglings of all four of these "elements." When they broke apart they recombined into different materials through the action of some ephemeral, cosmic force similar to Anaxagoras' Nous.

Democritus adopted and advanced Parmenides' thesis of the indestructibility of matter. He envisioned an infinite number of invisible, indivisible and indestructible units that he called atoms. These particles formed all matter and their aggregation and separation caused the changes observed in physical objects. Thus, when collisions between atoms occurred, those of irregular shape become entangled with one another to form groups of atoms and thus form the elements.

Twenty-one centuries later the English chemist, John Dalton, advanced the theory that combinations of extremely tiny, indivisible, and indestructible particles composed all elements. He recognizing the similarity of his theory to that advanced by Democritus and, in deference to Democritus, called them atoms.

Aristotle, a distinguished thinker and a close observer of nature, studied under Plato and tutored Alexander the Great. To his way of thinking, earth and heaven followed separate sets of natural law. On earth, each element had its own place; earth at the center followed by water, air and, highest of all, fire. An object composed mostly of earth would fall while air bubbles in water would rise. Rain fell but fire would rise.

His diligent inquiries into the causes of the whimsical and capricious weather led him to advance one grand theory that embraced all natural phenomena. He attempted to explain shooting stars, the aurora borealis, comets, halos, rainbows, the Milky Way, rain, clouds, mist, dew, frost, snow, hail, wind, rivers, seas, thunder, lightning, earthquakes, typhoons, fire-winds, and "thunderbolts."

Since he based his work on the then-accepted theory that four basic elements comprised the entire universe, most of his conclusions fail the test of modern investigation.

None the less, he and the early Greek philosophers, through the power of pure reasoning for they had only crude instruments, advanced the physical understanding of the earth, of medicine, mathematics, astronomy, physics and meteorology far beyond anything that had previously transpired. Their searches led them surprisingly close to such modern concepts as elements, atoms and the underlying force of pure energy.

Aristotle observed and wrote voluminously on all matters of philosophy and science. Most of his works disappeared in Europe after the fall of Rome but survived among the Arabs. During the 12th and 13th centuries AD, European Christians translated his books into Latin. The collection contains nearly a hundred and fifty volumes, a one-man encyclopedia of the knowledge of his times, which remained the authoritative source on scientific matters until the Scientific Revolution began in the 16th century.

AFTER THE GREEKS

Alexander's death marked the apex of Greek temporal power. After the Romans destroyed Carthage, their main competition, they turned their attention eastward. During the ensuing three centuries, Greek and Roman history blends into one. Together they produced the greatest civilization attained by Western Man until the discovery of the New World.

The Greeks exhibited an exceptional zeal to learn new things and an eagerness to pass their knowledge to all whom they met in their explorations. The Romans displayed a passion for law and order rather than knowledge and novelty. Although they quickly adopted innovative changes in administration, they evinced a remarkable lack of interest in technology and science. Consequently, scientific investigation diminished during the gradual collapse of the Greek world and the ascension of the Roman Empire. The Romans reverted largely to a more ancient, oriental, posture such as existed in Egypt and Asia.

In the 5th century, the Huns, Goths, Visigoths and Vandals laid waste to the Roman Empire, shattering that great social and economic culture into hundreds of small communities and leaving a once civilized and orderly world in chaos. Without any form of central authority, life became hard and dangerous -- often reduced to little more than an effort to survive. A Dark Age encroached upon the western world and practically all social and scientific progression stagnated for several centuries.

CHAPTER SIX

THE AGE OF TECHNOLOGY

Wherein we describe the tools, instruments and machines used to measure weather parameters -- and the renaissance and post-renaissance luminaries that invented them.

"The emphasis of Italian humanism on the glories of ancient literature and art made way for a less ethereal stress on current practical needs. Men had to count and calculate, measure and design, with competitive accuracy and speed; they needed tools of observation and recording; demands arose which were met by the invention of logarithms, analytical geometry, calculus, machines, the microscope, the telescope, statistical methods, navigational guides, and astronomical instruments. Throughout Western Europe lives were henceforth dedicated to meeting these needs."
-- Durant and Durant

THE RENAISSANCE

Considering the impact weather and climate have had on human evolution and development, it comes as little surprise that much early scientific research focused on the atmosphere and its weather. Before meteorology emerged as a separate academic interest in the late 1800s, atmospheric investigation continuously drew into its fold scientists of widely different backgrounds and interests. Throughout the ages, philosophers, researchers and experimenters from every scientific field contributed to the advancement of meteorological knowledge.

The development of three basic instruments during the technological renaissance -- the thermometer, the barometer and the hygrometer -- allowed investigators at last to measure the more immediately important properties of weather. Other instruments destined to transform meteorology into a true science would, in time, follow.

In the first century AD, the Greek engineer, Hero, used a very simple instrument to demonstrate that air had substance. He placed an open container upside-down into a tank of water. The air trapped within prevented water from filling the container until he allowed the air to bubble out. From this he concluded that air had material substance.

Philo of Byzantium, in the second century BC, proved that air expands when heated. He attached one end of a bent tube to a hollow lead globe, placed the other end into a flask of water, and set the apparatus in the sun. As the air in the lead flask warmed, some escaped from the tube and bubbled up through the water in the flask. When he took the apparatus into the shade, the lead globe cooled and the water level in the flask fell.

Philo concluded that the sun's heat expanded the air in the lead globe and forced some out through the tube. The loss of air inside the lead globe formed a partial vacuum, which allowed water to rise from the flask into the tube when the globe cooled.

THE AGE OF EXPERIMENTATION

These crude apparatuses, probably the world's first barometer and thermometer, proved that air has substance and expands when heated. These instruments could not, however, gauge the weight of the air nor the degree of temperature increase and thus failed the modern test of instrumentation -- the ability to measure.

Modern meteorology embraces the physics, chemistry, thermodynamics and hydrodynamics of the atmosphere and investigates the direct effects of weather upon the earth's surface and life in general. Today's meteorologists know that a mixture of gaseous atoms and molecules -- plus water vapor, dust and industrial pollutants -- comprise the earth's atmosphere. Movements of moist air heated by the sun generates the weather which we can forecast with a certain degree of accuracy. However, without the instruments that would come some thirteen hundred years later, the Greek philosophers could hardly have advanced science further than they did.

The Renaissance, born in Italy during the 15th century, marked the closing of the Middle Ages with its preoccupation with theology and the afterworld. In its stead there awoke a new era -- one in which interest in Man and the secular world would spark an astounding revolution in art, literature, architecture and commerce.

The Renaissance spread inexorably to northern Europe approaching its zenith in the 16th century. The following century proved one of the most productive periods in the history of science. Mathematicians, chemists, physicists and astronomers, who performed most of the early atmospheric research, introduced a new kind of philosophy -- the inductive method of reasoning based on observation -- and thus laid the foundations of modern thought. They also developed and refined the primary instruments -- the thermometer, the barometer and the hygrometer -- necessary to conduct a scientific study of the atmosphere.

THE BAROMETER

Aristotle's theory that "nature abhors a vacuum" had persisted to the 15th century despite the fact that experimenters and engineers had produced partial vacuums in cylinders and developed vacuum pumps that could raise water from one level to another.

Otto von Guericke, a German physicist, intrigued by the apparent paradox, decided to settle the question through experimentation rather than philosophical argument. He invented the first air pump, a reasonably airtight piston that operated within a cylinder, with which he evacuated the air from vessels. He demonstrated that candles would not burn and animals could not live within the evacuated vessel, thus proving that a vacuum existed.

Even the most efficient vacuum pump, however, could not raise water higher than about 33 feet. Torricelli, at the urging of Galileo, investigated the problem and, in so doing, invented the barometer. Torricelli, knew that air had weight. He decided that a raised piston reduced the pressure inside a water pump, allowing the weight of air pushing on the surface of the water to force it upward and fill the vacuum. To check his theory, he filled a four-foot glass tube with mercury and inverted it into a dish of mercury. The mercury in the "Torricelli Tube" settled only slightly leaving a near-perfect vacuum at the top of the tube (the Torricelli vacuum). He concluded that the weight of the atmosphere, pressing on the dish of mercury, balanced the weight of the mercury in the tube and prevented it from flowing out completely.

René Descartes applied the first scale to a Torricelli tube and used it to measure atmospheric pressure differences and Robert Boyle gave the barometer its name (from the Greek words báros (weight) and métron (measure).

Blaise Pascal, in 1645, demonstrated that the atmosphere thins with height by persuading his younger brother to walk a barometer to the summit (3458 feet) of Puy de Dôme in the Auvergne mountains. During the ascent, the mercury level in the tube fell 3.33 inches -- a dynamic illustration that atmospheric pressure decreases with height.

Much later, in 1843, Lucien Vidie invented the aneroid barometer, a metal bellows that contracts or expands as the atmospheric pressure rises or falls. The compact and easily transportable design permitted researchers to carry barometers to mountain tops and up in balloons to investigate the characteristics of air above the immediate surface.

THE THERMOMETER

Beginning with Galileo's "thermoscope" in 1593, the thermometer passed through a century of modifications while experimenters, including such luminaries as Robert Boyle and Isaac Newton, tried a wide variety of materials, scales and calibration schemes. Finally, in 1714, Gabriel Daniel Fahrenheit settled on mercury for the liquid indicator and consolidated the many inconsistent scaling schemes into one that gained permanent popularity. Although not English, he selected a scale based on the number twelve (suggested by Newton) and multiplied the base number by eight to get a range of 96 gradations on the scale. He assigned zero degrees to the lowest temperature he could obtain by cooling a mixture of water and salt, and 96 degrees to the normal heat of the human body. Subsequent experiments fixed the freezing point of pure water at 32 degrees and the boiling point at 212 degrees. On this revised scale the human body temperature became 98.6 degrees.

On the simpler, centigrade, scale (recently renamed Celcius in honor of Anders Celcius), ice melts at zero degrees and pure water boils at 100 degrees. Scientists prefer this scale, based on the number ten rather than on the number twelve, because it facilitates calculations.

The Fahrenheit scale, however, remains popular with lay persons in this country. The numbers on the Fahrenheit scale have specific meanings developed through years of association with warm and cold experiences. Everyone knows what a sticky 100 degree afternoon feels like. But it takes a deliberate effort to associate a temperature of 38 degrees Celcius (100°F) with a hot sultry summer day.

THE HYGROMETER

When humans acquired language, they also gained the ability to name natural phenomena. This led to the concept of association and thus to objective (scientific) analysis. With names they could, and ultimately did, associate water with rain, rain with clouds and, by association, water with clouds. They observed and named various forms of airborne water such as dew, mist, steam, clouds and fog and instinctively concluded that air somehow contained water.

Ancient sailors collected drinking water at sea by hanging sheepskins about the ship. Water vapor condensed on the wool during the night. In the morning, sailors stripped the dew from the skins into barrels to use for drinking and cooking.

Leonardo da Vinci designed, but did not build, a hygrometer that would measure the amount of moisture in the air. In his design, a delicate scale balanced a cotton swatch against a piece of wax. The cotton absorbed moisture and become heavier while the wax did not. The earliest hygrometers used the absorptive properties of cotton, wool, paper, wood or human hair to measure the moisture contained in the air.

In the 18th century, scientists discovered that the water contained in the air did not exist as minute droplets but rather as invisible molecules of water (actually a gas which we call water vapor and discern as humidity). Thus, water exists as an atmospheric gas as well as a liquid and a solid. Water vapor forms, at most, about five percent of the total air mass but it represents an almost indescribably vital constituent of the ecosphere. Additionally, as 19th century atmospheric scientists discovered, water vapor fuels the mighty storms that rage across our continent and around the world.

THE ANEMOMETER

The Greeks called the wind *anemos*. Thus we call an instrument used to measure wind speed an anemometer. Early sailors used the effects of the wind on the ships rigging to estimate its force. A small flag placed on the top of the highest mast gave the helmsman the direction of the wind, although he could only estimate the actual speed.

Leon Battista Alberti, elaborating on a simple natural indicator, built, or at least described, the first man-made instrument for measuring windspeed. Things that hang tend to hang at an angle when the wind blows against them. Alberti formalized this concept by using a metal plate that could swing in the wind. The stronger the wind, the further from the vertical the plate would hang. A curved graduated scale placed next to the plate indicated the speed.

Humans can employ the pressure-plate concept to estimate very strong winds. In hurricane force winds, a person can lean so far into the wind that he or she can nearly touch the ground without falling.

In Texas, according to legend, they necessarily use a more rugged system -- a large hanging chain. A light wind moves the chain. A moderate wind forces the chain to a 45 degree angle and a strong wind forces it to a nearly horizontal position. When the wind becomes very strong, it begins to snap links off the end of the chain. So goes the story.

In the early days of aviation, before longer flights became possible, pilots merely assumed the wind would not change direction before they returned to land. When flying far distances, they had to determine the ground wind direction from blowing smoke and other natural indicators. Soon most airports set up a wind sock -- a conical shaped piece of cloth with the tip cut off and the large end attached to an iron ring that could pivot. The orientation of the sock gave pilots the direction of the wind and its shape provided an estimate of the wind's velocity.

John Robinson invented the cup anemometer in the 1800s. The cup anemometer uses three, sometimes four, small cones or cups, that rotate on a spindle. Wind fills the front of the cup and forces it around the spindle but exerts relatively less force on the conical or spherical backside. A recorder counts the number of turns per minute and converts the number into miles per hour. More advanced systems use a anemograph which continuously records the wind speed and direction on a chart.

KITES, BALLOONS AND AIRPLANES

From simple observation of cloud movements, early researchers knew that weather systems extended far up into the atmosphere. They knew also that observations taken on mountaintops could provide only limited knowledge of conditions above the surface. To get more detailed upper-air information, they employed a variety of novel vehicles such as manned and unmanned balloons, airplanes and kites.

In 1749 Alexander Wilson of the University of Glasgow made the first upper-air measurements using a chain of several kites. He attached thermometers to the tails of the kites to take measurements at several levels. Although it could ascend to only a few hundred feet, the kite remained for many years the only means to systematically measure wind speed in the upper atmosphere.

In 1783, Jean Francois Pilatre de Rozier of France made the first free balloon ascent. Meteorologists, who often harbor souls of adventurers and explorers, hastened to venture aloft in hot-air and hydrogen balloons, often to perilous heights, to make atmospheric observations. Just one year after the first flight, Dr. John Jeffries and aeronaut Jean Pierre François Blanchard went aloft in a hot-air balloon and recorded temperature, humidity and pressure up to 9000 feet.

In 1804, the French chemist, Gay-Lussac, brought back a sample of the air from a height of nearly 24 thousand feet. Between 1862 and 1866, English meteorologist James Glaisher made 29 flights during which he made atmospheric measurements up to 29,000 feet before succumbing and nearly dying from lack of oxygen.

While interesting and helpful, the fragmentary information gained through manned balloon ascents often proved inaccurate as well as infrequent. In the late 19th century many nations reintroduced the kite to supplement balloon observations. From 1895 until 1933 the U. S. Weather Bureau lofted instruments on kites to measure upper-air wind, temperature, humidity, and pressure.

The box kite provided the best combination of lifting power and stability. Depending on the situation, they flew one of three sizes -- High-Wind, Moderate-Wind, or Light-Wind models. The Moderate-Wind kite stood six feet, eight and one-half inches tall, six feet, five and one-half inches wide and two feet, eight and one-half inches deep. It weighed eight and one-half pounds and required two men to launch it. Strings of several box kites, tethered by piano wire, could lift a "Marvin Meteorograph" over 20,000 feet, taking measurements every 500 feet.

The Weather Bureau routinely made kite flights from Mount Weather in Virginia, and Blue Hill Observatory in Boston. For an observing network, however, they preferred a flatter terrain. ". . . the best location is one in level country rather than on a mountain top . . . as free as possible from forested tracts, lakes, marshes, rivers, etc.; also from towns, steam and electric railways, and high tension power lines . . ." Strong winds occasionally snapped the piano-wire tether. The breakaway kites would sail away across hill and dale carrying instruments dangling from several miles of piano wire. After chasers retrieved the rogue kite string, they tied it to the bumper of a model-T truck and flew it back to the station. The locality therefore required good roads so they could recover kites that broke away.

The "ideal" location perfectly described Ellendale, North Dakota, where my father, also an itinerant weather-man, flew kites for the Weather Bureau for several years before my birth.

Kite flying on a large scale contains elements of risk -- even disaster. Although well grounded, the tethering wire occasionally melted from lightning strikes. In August, 1919, one man, less fortunate than Ben Franklin, died from a surge of electricity coming down the wire.

In 1919, airplanes began making daily observations at Washington, D.C. and soon replaced the kite as the easiest way to obtain upper-air data. However, launching dozens of aircraft across the country to take simultaneous observations proved costly and dangerous. Between 1931 and 1938, 12 pilots died making weather observation flights.

The increase in aviation during the war generated a greater demand for "real-time" upper-air information. In response, the Weather Bureau allocated $100,000 to enlarge their network of kite stations.

ELECTRICITY -- AND THE TELEGRAPH

The invention of electromagnetism and the electric generator in the 19th century changed the world as extensively as the steam engine had changed it a century earlier. Electricity did more than provide a relatively cheap, convenient and easily obtainable source of heat, light and industrial power. It opened the way for high-speed, long-distance communications so vital to the development of meteorological theory and operations.

Since antiquity, humans have known the novelty of amber which, when rubbed, acquires an electrical charge that can attract small objects. In the 16th century, Gilbert discovered that many other substances contain this attractive electrical force. He grouped them together under the name of *electrics* (from the Greek word for amber, *elektron*).

Early in the 17th century, Otto von Guericke devised a frictional machine that could produce large electric sparks. Benjamin Franklin, during his famous kite-flying experiment, proved that thunderstorms produce natures own type of electricity in the form of lightning bolts. In the early 18th century Musschenbroek contrived the "Leyden jar," the first truly efficient device for storing static electricity. But Leyden jars and other condensers discharge their potential instantaneously and thus, while interesting, held little practical value outside the laboratory.

During the early part of the 19th century, Count Volta, the Italian physicist, invented the first electric battery. His "Voltac pile" produced a steady, *dynamic* current of electricity that experimenters quickly put to work. A generation later William Sturgeon and John Frederic Daniell began to produce successively better batteries that yielded stronger currents for much longer periods of time. These developments set the stage for the breakthrough in electrical power that would soon follow.

Hans Christian Oersted uncovered the relationship between an electrical current and magnetism when he showed that a current in a copper wire deflected a compass needle. Sturgeon, working with an iron coil and an electric current invented the first electromagnet -- a device soon greatly improved by Joseph Henry to the world's immense benefit.

Michael Faraday, struck by Oersted's experiments, began working with electromagnetism. Shortly he discovered that moving a magnet through a wire coil produced an electrical current. From this seminal discovery of electromagnetic inductance, Faraday quickly developed the electric generator wherein wires moving across magnetic lines of force produce an electric current. The electric generator sparked a new technological revolution based on electrical power rather than steam.

Joseph Henry, America's foremost scientist of the day, independently discovered the electromagnet about the same time as Faraday. During his experiments he found that, by opening and closing the current to an electromagnet, he could send (telegraph) a simple signal consisting of short and long pulses some distance over a wire.

The electric generator, producing much more power than batteries, increased the transmission distance of his telegraph signals. To overcome the resistance in wire that gradually erodes the flow of current over long distances, Henry invented an electric relay that could activate small power sources at points along the wire. The invention of the generator and the relay allowed Samuel Morse to build a practical telegraph that could send signals over very long distances -- an invention that would greatly facilitate the process of gathering weather data and ultimately transform meteorology into a theoretical science as well as a practical one.

Morse got most of his ideas for the telegraph from the now lesser-known Henry. But he did build (and copyright) the first telegraph and he did invent the Morse Code. He established the first telegraph line between Washington, D.C. and Baltimore over which he sent his famous message, "What hath God wrought?"

Henry quickly realized that he could use the telegraph to gather simultaneous weather observations from an area covering several states making it possible to define and track individual storms as they raced across the mid-western prairies.

THE RADIO

Not long after Heinrich Rudolf Hertz demonstrated the existence of electromagnetic waves (In 1888), Marchese Guglielmo Marconi saw the potential of using them as a signaling device. Before long he could generate an electromagnet wave that could cause a bell to ring thirty feet away. Over the next few years he increased the power of his signals and, in 1898, developed a commercial wireless system.

Popov, a Russian physicist, increased the range over which electromagnetic waves could be detected and devised the first antenna to boost reception. By 1897 he could send and receive a signal over a distance of three miles.

Marconi continued to improve the wireless and, in 1900, obtained the patent and became the official inventor of the radio. Although radio signals could not yet carry voice messages, his radio made a big hit during the 1904 World's Fair in St. Louis.

Until Reginald Aubrey Fressenden invented the modulator, however, radios could send only dot-dashes pulses such as morse code. The modulator impressed small variations in sound, such as music or the human voice, onto a continuous signal. Demodulators at a receiving station could detected the variations and reconvert them into the original sound.

In 1906, Lee De Forest, second only to Edison in the number of personal patents held, produced the triode. This device amplified weak radio signals, much as Henry's relay did for telegraph signals, and made radio, and a vast array of other electronic equipment as well, commercially practical. Soon after, the Weather Bureau began transmitting forecasts and warnings over radio.

As the telegraph transformed meteorology into a practical science, radio took it to a still higher level. Radio, unrestricted by wires, proved a much more practical means of acquiring observational data and disseminating weather forecasts than the telegraph.

In time, a device called the radiosonde, attached to a large balloon, would radio to earth accurate and detailed vertical measurements through the upper reaches of the atmosphere and provide a third, vitally important, dimension to atmospheric data.

THE RADIOSONDE

The radiosonde compacts a thermometer, a barometer, a hygrometer and a battery-powered radio into a box about eight inches square and four inches thick..

A large helium-filled balloon carries the radiosonde to heights exceeding 100,000 feet while ground observers track the instrument with a surveyor's telescope or a radio direction finder. The known ascent rate of the balloon, its angle above the horizontal and the time between observations provides the wind speed at various heights. This ingenious device radios temperature, pressure and moisture data to the ground station for pre-selected (standard) levels through the atmosphere.

As the radio transcended the wire systems for transmitting weather observations, the radiosonde transcended mountain top observatories and expensive airplanes as a means to measure the structure of the upper atmosphere. The increased volume of high-quality data from the expanded radiosonde network allowed meteorologists to map the atmospheric circulation at upper levels in great detail and determine the relationship between surface weather systems and the upper atmosphere.

The tremendous gains in atmospheric knowledge during the late 19th century, owed largely to improvements in data gathering techniques, led to rapid advancements in the theory of storm development during the early 20th century.

At the close of World War I, the Bergen School of Meteorology in Norway introduced their new concepts of air mass analysis. Although their conception hardly described all the complexities of the atmosphere, the Bergen weather model gave weather forecasters a useful facsimile of meteorological processes. Air mass analysis, with its cold fronts, cyclones and anticyclones, served the meteorology community well through the close of World War II. In modified form it still appears daily in newspaper weather columns and TV weather presentations.

MODERN METEOROLOGICAL INSTRUMENTS

Since World War II, scientists have developed and refined a dazzling array of ever more sophisticated devices to measure and transmit data, maps, charts and photographs. As always, Weather Service forecasters and researchers quickly adopt those that improve weather forecasting and dissemination of information to the public.

Radar, especially the more advanced doppler radar, weather satellites and computers stand out as important meteorological tools. Among new and improved instrumentation, the Weather Service's ground-based "wind profiler" measures speed and direction of high-altitude winds at 72 different levels every six minutes through the lower 10 miles of our atmosphere. Space-age sensors, flying on earth-orbiting satellites, can observe low-level wind patterns over remote water-covered areas such as oceans and large lakes.

These, and many other lesser known instruments and machines, have greatly aided the processes of weather data gathering and forecast distribution.

One can hardly overemphasize the importance of communications in the field of meteorology. Rapid dissemination of forecasts, especially, severe weather warnings, remains a vital function of the U. S. Weather Service. The development of fiber optics and digital data transmission promises to create yet another data-processing/communication revolution before the advent of the new millennium. The revolution continues.

CHAPTER SEVEN

BOYLE'S LAW
ADIABATIC CHANGES
LATENT HEAT AND STORMS

Wherein we see 18th century scientists, using the instruments invented in the 17th century, develop the physical laws that 19th century scientists would apply to the atmosphere and lay the theoretical foundations for modern, 20th century, meteorological science.

"Unlike the physicist who could collect his data under simplified conditions in the laboratory, the meteorologist was faced with a highly complex system of constantly interacting parts whose behavior was beyond his control."
-- Gisela Kutzbach

GAIA

The land and water surfaces of Earth, combined with living matter and air, form a huge assemblage that may be regarded as a single organism -- a living creature in its own right. James Lovelock calls this giant organism Gaia, after the Greek Earth-goddess. Air, the circulatory system of the living earth, uses the sun's energy to distribute life-sustaining heat and moisture to its extremities. The circulating air, in its many configurations, generates the turbulent features we call weather.

Weather develops within and moves about through the atmosphere -- a fact of nature known to Man since antiquity. But curious Man can not rest until he knows exactly how such things as clouds, rain, thunderstorms, tornadoes and other atmospheric activities actually come about. The ancients could sense and speculate upon the forces behind such spectacular atmospheric phenomena but, until the age of instrumentation and experimentation opened in the 16th century, they could not measure them. Thus, they could not fully understand them.

THE NEW PARADIGM

The ancient Greeks, had few instruments with which to gather solid physical information. They derived their remarkable conclusions through a process called "deductive" thinking. They first studied a phenomena and developed a premise. Then, based on the premise, arrived at a conclusion that defined the cause and effect of the phenomena.

As the renaissance gained momentum, scientists began to develop and use instruments to measure natural phenomena. Instrumentation led to experimentation and a new means of scientific investigation called the "inductive" method. In the inductive mode of research, investigators drew their conclusions from factual evidence (data) gathered through careful (measured) observation and experimentation.

Three principal instruments -- the barometer, the thermometer and the hygrometer -- gave renaissance researchers the tools they needed to probe the atmosphere and begin to reveal its elusive secrets. Ultimately, scientists of the 16th, 17th and 18th centuries, determined the elements that comprise the atmosphere, developed the special laws that govern its behavior and established the science of meteorology. Yet, deductive thinking remains a useful tool. In addition to painstaking work, advancement in scientific research often involves educated guesses, brilliant flashes of insight -- and more than a touch of serendipity.

17ᵀᴴ AND 18ᵀᴴ CENTURY GENIUSES

Scientifically, a perfect gas does not exist in a natural state.

Biologically, the atmosphere approximates a perfect gas because it evolved in symbiotic concert with the biosphere it supports. In turn, the biosphere conditions the atmosphere in ways that maintain this essential compatibility.

Meteorologically, our atmosphere, either dry or containing water vapor (and pollutants) closely approximates the behavior of a perfect gas.

By modern definition, a gas, perfect or not, must rigorously behave in a manner that follows the several laws developed by the 17th and 18th century experimental scientists, Boyle, Mariotte, Amontons, Charles, Gay-Lussac, Dalton, Avagadro, Kelvin, Carnot, Coriolis, Leibniz, Mayer, Helmholtz and Joule. Through careful laboratory experiments and mathematical analysis, these brilliant scientists developed the fundamental laws that describe gaseous behavior and thus form the basis of meteorological science.

Boyle, a 17th century physicist and chemist, first discovered that gases follow an inverse volume-to-pressure relationship while trying to improve vacuum pumps. He trapped a gas in the closed end of a seventeen-foot long tube and added mercury into the open end -- thus exerting pressure on the gas trapped in the end.

When he doubled the amount of mercury -- thus doubling the pressure -- the volume of the trapped gas reduced to one half the original volume. When he tripled the pressure, the volume dropped to one third and so forth. When he removed the pressure, the gas returned to its original volume. Convinced that air must consist of small particles that crowd together under pressure, Boyle joined the currently growing circle of atomists who believed that *all* matter consists of small, indestructible particles.

Mariotte, Boyle's French contemporary, added an important element to this fundamental law of meteorology. He noted that Boyle's pressure-to-volume relationship held true only under constant temperature. Under constant pressure, gases expand and contract as the temperature increases or decreases. Thus, when considering the behavior of a gas, one must consider the concurrent changes of all three parameters -- volume, pressure and temperature.

In the 17th and 18th centuries, Gay-Lussac and Dalton continued to investigate the Boyle-Mariotte gas law. In a classic experiment, Gay-Lussac allowed a gas to expand from one container into a second of equal size -- thus doubling the volume. He noted that, although he neither added nor subtracted heat during the process, the first chamber cooled as it lost pressure and the second chamber heated as it gained pressure.

Dalton expanded Boyle's concept of particles and volumes and determined that, again without addition or subtraction of external heat, the temperature of air increases when compressed and decreases when expanded - - the obverse of Gay Lussac's temperature-volume corollary. Meteorologists now call changes in volume and temperature of air, where no infusion of external heat or extraction of internal heat occurs, *adiabatic* processes.

Dalton acquired a keen and long-lasting interest in weather. Using homemade instruments, he amassed over 200,000 weather observations during nearly 60 years of atmospheric investigation. While studying the composition of air, he came to believe, as did Boyle, that the atmosphere, and, indeed, all matter, consists of tiny, indivisible and indestructible particles (which he named atoms). Further, he discovered that water almost invariably appears as one of the gaseous constituents of air. Moreover, he determined that the amount of water vapor that a parcel of air can hold increases with the temperature. Later investigations revealed that water contained in the air exists as molecules of gaseous vapor rather than minute particles of liquid water.

These essential discoveries laid the foundation of modern meteorology. In later centuries, atmospheric scientists would reformulate and expand these fundamental laws to learn how the atmosphere develops the high and low pressure systems that produce clear skies, wind, cyclonic storms and other atmospheric phenomena that we call weather.

WATER VAPOR AND LATENT HEAT

No amount of exaggeration can overstate the importance of water vapor to meteorological processes -- and to life on earth. Although water vapor forms at most about five percent of the total air mass, this marvelous gas, aided by radiation from the sun, transports vital heat and moisture from the oceans to the biosphere, controls the global atmospheric circulation and fuels the mighty storms that rage across our continent and around the world.

Most water vapor enters the air over the tropical oceans. Each day the sun beats down on the vast water surfaces of the tropics -- a belt some 3000 miles wide and 25,000 miles long. During the day, molecules of water, agitated by heat from the sun, escape (evaporate) from the ocean surface. They change state, from liquid water to gaseous water (water vapor), and pass into the surrounding air.

The heat required to liberate water molecules from the ocean surface remains with them as they float around the world on atmospheric currents. Meteorologists call this internal energy, *latent heat* -- from Greek and Latin meaning hidden or veiled. When water vapor transforms back into liquid water (condenses), it releases the latent heat it gained during evaporation and warms the surrounding air.

ENERGY, HEAT AND WORK --THE RUDIMENTS OF WEATHER

In the vernacular, the terms energy, heat and work commonly embody a wide range of activities and nuances. In the scientific world, however, these terms have precise definitions.

Scientists draw an important distinction between heat and temperature. They define the heat of a body as the kinetic energy of its constituent particles (atoms and molecules) and the temperature of the body as simply a convenient measure of the body's internal kinetic energy -- sometimes called its heat intensity.

A classic experiment illustrates the difference between temperature and heat. Five marbles, all of the same size but made of different materials (lead, glass, zinc, brass and iron), are heated in boiling water to a temperature of 100°C and, at a given instant, placed on a thin sheet of paraffin. The iron and brass marbles quickly melt their way through the wax but the lead and glass marbles never do.

The iron and brass marbles, although raised to the same temperature as the others, acquired more heat than the glass and lead marbles. Iron and brass therefore have a greater capacity to hold heat (greater specific heat) than lead or glass.

The concept of specific heat becomes meteorologically important when considering the effect of water vapor on the ecosphere. Water vapor has a much greater specific heat than dry air. Therefore, although moist air may have the same temperature as dry air, moist air always contains a much greater quantity of heat. Even cold air contains heat in the form of water vapor. Water vapor carries heat and moisture from the warm tropical oceans to the cold polar regions and thus maintains an equitable climate over much of the earth.

James Joule discovered the close relationship between work and heat and energy conversion. His experiments showed conclusively that the work performed on a system always produced a particular quantity of heat. He calculated that 41,800,000 ergs of work produced one calorie of heat -- a figure he called the "mechanical equivalent of heat."

During the 1840s and 1850s, scientists enfolded the concepts of heat and energy conversion into the basic laws of thermodynamics. These laws, which profoundly advanced the science of meteorology, state that, while mechanical motion (kinetic energy) can generate heat and, conversely, heat (potential energy) can generate mechanical motion, neither can create or destroy energy. Both forms of energy can, when properly employed, perform work. Meteorologists restrict the definition of work to processes wherein a volume of air gains or loses heat (potential energy) as it expands or contracts against the surrounding pressure field.

During the 19th century, researchers from many fields of science applied the universal laws of thermodynamics and hydrodynamics to the behavior of air and water vapor. As they gradually added scientific theory to existing practical (applied) meteorology, they came to understand how changes in pressure, caused by changes in air temperature, place the atmosphere in motion to produce weather.

CHAPTER EIGHT

MODERN METEOROLOGY
THE EARLY YEARS

Wherein we describe the development and early applications of "synoptic" meteorology and the "art" of weather forecasting.

"Whatever may be the progress of the sciences, never will observers who are trustworthy and careful of their reputations venture to forecast the state of the weather."
  -- Dominique Arago, 17th century French physicist

WEATHER FORECASTING -- A LESSON IN HUMILITY

British Vice Admiral Robert Fitzroy ignored Arago's sage advice. As a seaman, Fitzroy knew that current conditions can foretell coming weather -- a principle he felt to be valid over land as well as sea. In 1861, under the auspices of the Royal Society, he established a network of 22 observing stations along the coasts of France and the British Isles. Collecting simultaneous weather observations from the network via telegraph, he analyzed the current weather as it blew in from the Atlantic Ocean and issued daily forecasts and storm warnings based on approaching storms.

He forecasted wind and rain 48 hours in advance with variable success and, for his efforts, drew criticism from all sides. *The Times* printed Fitzroy's forecasts but, after one particularly unsuccessful week, felt obligated to include a caveat: "While disclaiming all credit for the occasional success, we must however demand to be held free of any responsibility for the too common failures which attend these prognostications. During the last week Nature seems to have taken special pleasure in confounding the conjectures of science."

Evidently, Fitzroy, who suffered frequent bouts of depression under normal conditions, weakened under the harsh criticism of his project. In April, 1865, he committed suicide -- a tragic end to the career of one of the world's earliest operational weather forecasters.

As meteorologists would later appreciate, the coarseness of the observation grid proved a major factor in Fitzroy's failure. Similar weather observing and forecasting networks, established in the 1850s and 60s by Buys Ballot in the Netherlands and Urbain LaVernier in France, met with similar lack of success.

EARLY AMERICAN METEOROLOGISTS

Joseph Henry, the erstwhile inventor of the telegraph, became the first director of the Smithsonian Institute. Henry, who believed that "man is a meteorologist by nature," had a penchant for weather. He astutely observed that the vast mid-western plains of the United States constituted a natural laboratory for the study and advancement of meteorology.

This expanse of level terrain lies between 30 degrees and 50 degrees north -- exactly the latitudes where dry polar and moist tropical air masses meet in perennial conflict. Moreover, nothing stands between cold Canadian polar air and the prairie states but a few strands of wire fence, and nothing blocks the flow of humid, tropical air from the Gulf of Mexico into the plains of the southeastern and Midwestern states. When these contrasting air masses meet and mingle, they generate some of the world's most explosive and spectacular storms.

This region, 1500 miles on a side, can contain complete storm systems. Forecasters and researchers can follow storms as they develop and move across the flat plains and prairies from the Rockies to the Atlantic Ocean. Even the low range of the Appalachians offers but a small obstacle to storms passing over this relatively uniform surface.

Henry established a network of weather observers stationed along the rapidly spreading telegraph wires, and turned meteorology into a truly practical science. Telegraph operators made systematic synchronous weather observations (using instruments supplied by Henry) and relayed them to the Smithsonian. By 1861, operators at 600 telegraph stations made and transmitted regular weather observations. In short time other visionaries such as Cleveland Abbe and James Pollard Espy also developed weather networks covering several states in the mid-west.

At the Smithsonian Castle, Henry plotted pressure, temperature and wind data on the world's first weather maps and displayed them in the great hall. This "synoptic" view of the nation's weather provided by the synchronous weather observations made it possible to locate storms and follow their movement. By extrapolating a storm's past movement, meteorologists could make simple forecasts of impending weather.

Cleveland Abbe, then Director of Cincinnati's Mitchell Astronomical Observatory, began publishing a simple *Weather Bulletin* for Cincinnati in 1869. His observation network totaled 36 stations of which only 10 lay west of Cincinnati -- the direction from whence virtually all major storms approached. His westernmost observations came from Omaha, Nebraska and Fort Levenworth, Kansas, barely 600 miles to the west. Since major storms can easily travel that distance in one day, it required extreme diligence to spot them in time to make a useful forecast.

Since Abbe's sparse network of observations could barely define approaching storm systems, his forecasts often failed. Additionally, as weather forecasters everywhere would quickly discover, storms often did not, and still do not, necessarily behave in an orderly fashion.

Henry's weather maps displayed in the great hall of the Smithsonian quickly became a popular gathering place for Washington, D. C. residents. Henry made weather forecasts for Smithsonian activities and private individuals but he refused to make public forecasts or storm warnings. In his mind, the government should provide such services and recommended that the United States place all meteorological operations under one agency "as an effective means of predicting storms and warning coastal shipping."

THE U.S. WEATHER BUREAU

Military communications overburdened the telegraph service during the Civil War and temporarily halted meteorological services to the public. After the war, however, Congress proposed, and, in 1870, President Ulysses S. Grant signed a resolution to establish a national weather service under the auspices of the U. S. Army Signal Service.

The new weather bureau focused primarily on service to agriculture, shipping and other weather-sensitive industries. The War Department, however, concerned that Signal Service duties as weather observers and forecasters might jeopardize military capabilities in times of emergency, became convinced that weather services should not be a military function. The congress agreed and, on July 1, 1891, transferred the embryonic weather bureau, including all weather stations, telegraph lines, personnel (honorably discharged) and equipment, to the Department of Agriculture.

Interest in weather forecasts for agriculture and other commerce impelled a continuous expansion of the weather observing network. In 1903, the Wright brothers' historic first airplane flights presaged a shift in emphasis followed by an ever increasing need for weather services. Within ten years of the first flights, growing demands from the aviation industry forced the Weather Bureau to add an aerology section to its growing list of services. Within a short time, service to aviation occupied a major portion of the services provided by the Weather Bureau.

In the early 1900s, the "wireless" (radio) emerged as the most important new meteorological tool since the telegraph. Atmospheric scientists, frequently among the first to apply new inventions to science, quickly saw the usefulness of the radio. No longer constrained to narrow strips along telegraph lines, observers could radio their observations from mountain tops, deserts, jungles and oceans -- virtually anywhere on earth *to* anywhere on earth. As well as adding the observational density necessary to define large-scale weather systems, this vastly expanded capability added a new dimension to the vital process of disseminating forecasts and warnings to the public. Soon after the radio appeared, the Weather Bureau began receiving observations from and sending forecasts to ships at sea and exchanging weather data with Russia and eastern Asia as well as Europe.

THE ART OF FORECASTING

At the beginning of the 20th century scientists had developed an impressive array of conceptual theories concerning storm development and movement. Little of this knowledge, however, reached down to influence the typical forecaster who acquired his skills through on-the-job training and experience.

Usually, meteorologists made forecasts by extrapolating the pressure patterns appearing on their weather maps. They forecasted a storm's movement according to recent pressure changes, wind directions, past storm tracks, numerous rules peculiar to the region and a good deal of inspired intuition.

In 1916, several of the more imminent forecasters of the day compiled their accumulated forecasting rules into a pamphlet that detailed "the processes by which good forecasts can be made." Unfortunately, sparsely distributed surface observations, very limited upper-air data, still primitive concepts of weather processes and varying climate influences presented a forecasting challenge too formidable to succumb to the application of a few empirical rules -- and exceptions to the rules.

Later, as forecasters gained experience, they experimented with weather analogs. They found a past situation that resembled the current one and assumed (hoped) the present weather would evolve in a manner similar to the historical event.

Experienced forecasters used the analog with modest success but many found it quite difficult to apply. Although weather systems occasionally appeared identical to previous episodes, they rarely unfolded in exactly the same manner. Even such common storms as the "Alberta Clipper," which form over Canada's Alberta Province in winter and race eastward to New England, often provided frustrating surprises for analog forecasters.

In 1969, Lorenz, who developed the theory of meteorological chaos, published an analysis of analogs. He demonstrated mathematically that true analogs rarely occur and, even with close matches, the weather does not exactly follow the analog. His analysis, and the surging successes of modern numerical forecasts, ended any lingering dependence on analog forecasting methods.

Frontal Assault

During the 19th century, American and European meteorologists gradually developed a good deal of fundamental theory and a number of practical weather-forecasting techniques. As often happens, however, a crisis accelerates the advancement of science.

Under the pressure of World War I, a team of Norwegian meteorologists, directed by visionary Jacob Bjerknes, developed a revolutionary new concept of cyclone storm structure and movement -- and initiated the truly practical application of meteorological science to everyday affairs.

During World War I, the Germans used dirigibles to bomb London. To deprive the Germans of the data they needed to make forecasts for their weather sensitive Zeppelins, England and the United States stopped general dissemination of weather data over the Atlantic Ocean. This, unfortunately, deprived Norway of the data they needed to forecast weather for their great fishing fleet. To compensate, the Norwegians organized a dense network of farmers, fishermen, lighthouse keepers and sailors along their west coast to observe weather and detect approaching storms. Bjerknes, and his colleges at Norway's Bergen School of Meteorology, processed the data and made the weather forecasts.

Their closely spaced observations soon revealed complexities in cyclones and other weather features that had thus far gone undetected. They learned that precipitation from a cyclone developed not from the low pressure itself but rather from the discontinuity between cold air thrusting down from the north into a tongue of warm air pushing northward into the storm's center. They termed this line of convergence between the cold and warm air the "squall line."

The Norwegians incorporated their new findings with the disparate parts of existing empirical weather knowledge and meteorological theory and developed the polar front/air mass concept of storm development. Couched in terms borrowed from the war, they described cold, dry air masses from the north invading warm, moist air masses in the south. They advanced the analogy further by portraying the "front" of the invading cold as a blue line with sharp prongs. The weaker, warm air masses, where they managed to encroach upon the cold air, appeared as red lines with soft rounded protrusions.

This seemingly simple, two-dimensional abstraction -- in which mid-latitude cyclones form along the boundary between polar and sub-tropical air masses -- brought order out of the apparent chaos of weather systems. The Bjerknes-Bergen model provided a practical schematic that forecasters still use to conveniently portray and follow moving weather systems. Examples of this ingenious and enduring weather model appear daily in newspapers and on television.

METEOROLOGICAL WORKS OF ART

Metaphors often serve to clarify things not easily seen or understood. The most important meteorological processes go unseen in our transparent atmosphere. To "observe" atmospheric changes, meteorologists must use instruments. To illustrate and vivify the complex motions that generate our weather they employ a vast array of symbolic images and metaphoric analogies.

The Norwegians developed a clever five-digit code that allowed observers to summarize both visual and numerical weather information into a short telegraphic message. Experienced meteorologists could glance at an incoming observation and actually "see" the weather at the reporting station. To aid visualization of weather over larger regions, they plotted the data on a map using pictorial symbols to illustrate various facets of the weather at each station.

Plotted by hand in an area about the size of a dime, these ingenious symbols contained vivid descriptions of the weather at reporting stations. Meteorologists could tell at a glance the wind, pressure, temperature, humidity, clouds, and precipitation occurring at major cities across the country and, by extrapolation, areas between.

Analysts quickly combined these station data into a larger metaphor, brimming with additional symbols including wind and pressure patterns, fronts, isotherms, areas of rapidly changing pressure as well as descriptions of clouds and various aspects of current weather.

Color added richness to the charts. Blue and red "fronts" portrayed the chaotic zone of turbulent weather between conflicting cold and warm air masses. A red "H" marked regions of high pressure, indicating generally clear skies and fair weather, whereas a blue "L" marked areas of low pressure, usually indicating cloudy, stormy conditions. They used green, with imbedded stars, dots, and inverted commas, to represent areas of snow, rain, and drizzle, and yellow to delineate foggy areas. To the trained eye, the completed map described at once the cause and effects of unfolding weather systems.

During the intervening years, before computers took over, meteorologists lofted weather-map analysis to a state of high art, replete with symbolic metaphor as well as texture, line and form. The uninitiated might easily have confused a well drawn weather map with a work of abstract art -- possibly a Miro.

THE NEW METEOROLOGY

The air mass/polar front theory bridged the rather wide gulf between the theoretical meteorologist and the practical weather forecaster. This new, improved, model provided the basis for further theoretical studies as well as practical applications to weather forecasting.

Subsequent to the war, the meteorological community, led by the brilliant Norwegians and aided by a steadily increasing flow of upper-air data, developed ever more comprehensive explanations of the complex vertical motions and pressure changes associated with cyclone development and movement.

CHAPTER NINE

THE THEORY OF METEOROLOGY

Wherein we unfold the history of meteorological theory. Here we see atmospheric scientists of the 19th and early 20th centuries utilize the increased frequency and accuracy of meteorological observations, in particular those of the upper air, and apply physical laws developed in the 17th and 18th century to the atmosphere to provide the theoretical foundations of modern meteorological science. We document further the development and early applications of "synoptic" meteorology and the "air-mass/frontal boundary" theory of meteorology.

"Dynamic meteorology starts from pure physical theory and attempts to give a systematic and quantitative description of the composition and physical behavior of the atmosphere. The goal is the complete explanation in physical terms of the atmospheric phenomena constituting the weather."
--Jörgen Holmboe

WEATHER -- A UNIVERSAL PREOCCUPATION

Almost no one feigns disinterest in the weather. The fervor and abiding interest in weather ensnares the sophisticated and ingenuous alike, crossing all artificial boundaries of race, creed and political persuasion. This perhaps explains why meteorological science has continuously drawn into its fold investigators of such widely different backgrounds and interests. Before meteorology emerged as a separate academic field in the late 1800s, researchers from every scientific area -- philosophy, physics, chemistry, mathematics, engineering and biology -- contributed to the understanding and advancement of meteorological theory.

Louis Gay-Lussac, Siméon Poisson and John Dalton, along with Isaac Newton, developed the basic theoretical tools necessary to elevate meteorology beyond simple descriptive accounts of unusual weather phenomena in the 18th century. As the 19th century opened, the burgeoning field of meteorology showed no want of capable investigators anxious to resolve the perplexing mysteries of the atmosphere. Still, it took nearly 100 years of enterprising research to advance weather science from a descriptive, anecdotal, status in the 1820s to the "breakthrough" in modern meteorological theory orchestrated by Vilhelm Bjerknes and his colleagues at the Bergen School of Meteorology in Norway.

Under Bjerknes leadership, the Norwegians merged the accumulated body of meteorological theory with their own research and, employing a novel descriptive approach, developed the wave or polar front theory of cyclones. Their model successfully explained the (then known) interacting forces and energy conversion processes occurring within developing and moving cyclones. The continued use today of the Bjerknes "polar front" model attests to the ingenuity and practicality of its design..

To Study a Storm

Imagine standing upon a small knoll in some mid-western state some 150 years ago watching an afternoon storm brew on the western horizon. You feel compelled to watch and study this storm so as to understand how it formed, why it moves, where it goes and how long it lasts. But, how and where to start?

In the distance you see a bank of clouds forming. You watch them rise to incredible altitudes -- sometimes as high as 60 thousand feet -- where they spread out westward into a thin veil that dims the sun. What, you wonder, causes these clouds to form? From whence comes the energy to propel them so rapidly upward and outward?

At closer hand, darker clouds, illuminated by frequent discharges of electricity, blot the sun from the sky. What, you ask, causes the fierce and often dangerous bolts of electricity to dart from cloud to cloud and from cloud to the ground?

The wind, becoming increasing strong and gusty, blows toward the storm's center. The rapidly upward moving air at the storm core has created a vacuum into which surrounding air rushes to fill. Judging from the high-level cloud movements, air spills out at the top of the storm and spreads laterally outward. Oddly, the cloud movement indicates that the outflowing air moves only in a westerly direction. Why would the air not flow outward in all directions equally? What connection exists between the surface circulation and the apparent westerly flow at higher elevations?

As the storm nears, the clouds lower, the wind becomes increasingly strong and gusty and rain begins to pelt down. As the storm passes, the wind switches into the north, the barometer fluctuates, and the temperature and humidity invariably drop.

These tumultuous activities, however, reveal only fragments of the thermodynamic processes proceeding concurrently, and in concert, within and above the storm. Clearly it will require a exceedingly large amount of surface and upper-air data to fully describe -- and ultimately to understand -- the complexity of a cyclonic storm system.

LOW PRESSURE AND STORMS

In the early 1800s, existing data with which to study storms consisted of little more than descriptive, anecdotal accounts of storms, complemented by widely scattered, frequently less than accurate, weather observations. Upper-air data consisted of that gleaned from mountain tops, the occasional balloon ascent and observations of cloud movements. Even by mid-nineteenth century their existed no systematic means by which to gather meteorological data.

The invention of the telegraph, which provided near-instantaneous, long-range communications, dramatically changed that situation. As telegraph lines rapidly spread through the Midwestern plains, visionaries such as Joseph Henry, Cleveland Abbe and James Pollard Espy each developed weather observing networks covering several states.

They gathered and plotted simultaneous weather observations taken by telegraph operators and analyzed the pressure, temperature and wind fields on large maps of the eastern United States. Using this pictorial view of the various weather elements, they quickly learned to correlate low and high pressure systems with certain types of weather. In a logical next step, they began first to track cyclonic storms as they moved across the continent then to forecast their movements. Ultimately they began to try to forecast their development.

Their forecasts failed as often as not owing mainly to insufficient data but also to a woefully inadequate knowledge of the atmospheric forces at work. Barometric measurements might reveal an area of low pressure, indicating an incipient storm system, but no one as yet understood the complex thermodynamic energy conversions that occur within the violent storms that rage across the Midwestern states and into the eastern seaboard.

A truly comprehensive theory of storm behavior had to await a more extensive observation network -- one that included the ability to observe air movements in the upper reaches of the atmosphere -- and a better understanding of the fundamental physical laws that determine the behavior of the gases comprising the earth's atmosphere.

ENTER THEORY

During the middle decades of the nineteenth century, three American scientists -- James Pollard Espy, William Ferrel and Elias Loomis -- formulated the "thermal theory" of cyclonic storm development. Their relatively simple theory incorporated many of the observed relationships between pressure, temperature and precipitation and provided a reasonable, although incomplete, explanation of the origin and behavior of cyclones.

In the early 1800s, Espy, a teacher of classical languages and mathematics, took an avid interest in meteorology -- specifically the relationship between rain and the quantity of water vapor contained in the air. This initial interest expanded into a general study of storms and, by mid-century, Espy stood as one of America's foremost experts on cyclone development.

It takes an extraordinary reach of intuition to perceive similarities between the formation of clouds caused by large-scale air currents in the free atmosphere and laboratory experiments with water vapor. But Espy had read Boyle, Dalton and Gay-Lussac and he had observed the puffy cumulus clouds that form on warm summer days.

He hypothesized that, on occasion, air near the surface of the earth becomes heated and rises -- much like bubbles in a pan of boiling water. He further surmised that the rising columns of ascending air carried with them water vapor and therefore latent heat acquired earlier through the process of evaporation.

Espy knew that air pressure decreases with height. The upper part of a rising air column would, therefore, rise to levels of lesser pressure and expand, causing the column to grow cooler. As the rising thermal cooled to its dew point temperature, molecules of water vapor within the thermal would condense into minute water droplets from which clouds would form.

He further conjectured that no significant external heat would enter or leave the current of air as it rose through the surrounding atmosphere. Therefore, only *adiabatic* temperature changes should occur within the air column.

To demonstrate his theory, Espy devised an instrument he called the nepheloscope, or cloud examiner. The instrument allowed him to measure the degree of cooling of dry or moist air as it expands. For a given expansion, and a resultant reduction in pressure, the moist air in the nepheloscope cooled to its dew point temperature and water vapor condensed out of the air -- a process analogous to the formation of clouds in a current of ascending air.

As a molecule of water vapor condenses into liquid water it releases the latent heat it acquired during evaporation. The increase in temperature causes the thermal column to expand even more, thus maintaining its upward motion. This process, Espy suggested, warmed the region and lowered the pressure over a field of rising thermals, causing cyclonic storms to develop. Air, accumulating above the storm through upward vertical convection, spread outward along the periphery causing higher pressure to surround the developing storm center.

Espy further noted that surface air, flowing inward towards the low pressure center to replace air depleted by rising thermals, moves in a spiral, anti-clockwise, motion. Since higher pressure surrounding the storm should push air more or less directly toward the center of low pressure, the circular flow and the tendency to spiral inward remained a mystery. A full generation later William Ferrell would recognize that a combination of a "deflecting" force caused by the earth's rotation and the frictional force generated by air flowing over the earth's surface produced and maintained the gyratory inflow of large-scale cyclones.

Espy's experiments linked adiabatic cooling and heating processes with thermal convection to provide a convincing explanation of cloud formation and storm development. But Espy had his detractors, among them William Redfield, America's prominent investigator of storms, and Heinrich Wilhelm Dove, Europe's most influential meteorologist of the day. Dove attributed storm development to currents of polar air displacing currents of equatorial air, with clouds and rain occurring through mechanical mixing of air within the two currents. He recognized no rotative wind circulation except in tropical storms. Redfield recognized the circular nature of storms but attributed the lower pressure to a depletion of air by through the centrifugal force generated by the storm's rotation.

Most researchers, including Ferell and Loomis, embraced Espy's postulate: Release of latent heat, through condensation of water vapor in vertically ascending currents, provided the immense power required for storms to develop. Still, no one knew exactly how the storms got started, what propelled them across the countryside or how they maintained their fury intact for several days.

Espy's endeavors predated the introduction of the first law of thermodynamics to meteorological science. Although he could determine experimentally the temperature changes and heat released during condensation of water vapor, he could not hope to calculate the potential power available for storm development lying over a million square-mile area of mid-western prairie. Such calculations depended on the concepts of energy conservation and the interchangeability of energy, heat and work introduced a generation later.

OUR TURBULENT (BUT STABLE) ATMOSPHERE

In the free atmosphere below the tropopause, the temperature decreases with height at a certain rate -- called the environmental lapse rate. The lapse rate depends on the local climatic regime and current weather conditions but, in general, it approaches 3.5°F per 1000 feet in moist air and 5.5°F per 1000 feet in dry air. Meteorologists also define several other lapse rates that describe special or idealized atmospheric conditions or atmospheric processes.

The munificent flow of energy from the sun causes our atmosphere to churn continuously. Yet, considering the amount of agitation, ranging in scale from tiny molecular eddies to broad flows of 300 miles per hour within jet streams, the air remains remarkably stable. Meteorologists call this seemingly paradoxical situation -- a churning stability -- hydrostatic stability or, sometimes, convective stability.

When a parcel of air becomes warmed by whatever means, it expands, becomes less dense than its surroundings and begins to rise. Once the parcel begins to rise, it encounters lower pressure and continues to expand and cool. However, it also encounters a new environment of cooler surrounding air. Whether the parcel continues to expand and rise or sinks back to its original level depends on the environmental lapse rate it encounters during its rise.

In an unstable atmosphere, the rising parcel cools less rapidly than the environment through which it passes. It thus remains warmer than its surroundings and continues to rise. If a rising air parcel cools to its dew point temperature, water vapor begins to condense into minute water droplets and clouds form. The concurrent release of latent heat prevents the rising parcel from cooling as rapidly as before which increases its buoyancy.

Most of the time, thermals cool more rapidly than the environment, lose their buoyancy and cease to rise. In convectively stable air, thermal agitation from local heating occurs only in the lower few thousand feet. Under these conditions, afternoon thermals may produce a field of low cumulus clouds but not large rain-producing cumulonimbus.

EMPIRICAL ART -- OR PHYSICAL SCIENCE?

Meteorology consists of two main disciplines; synoptic meteorology and dynamic meteorology.

Synoptic meteorologists use weather observations and attempt to describe graphically the current state of the weather. They then attempt to forecast changes in the weather from current developments and an empirical knowledge of cyclone behavior. Dynamic meteorologists have the same goal as synoptic meteorologists but proceed in quite a different manner. They attempt to describe and explain the physical behavior of the atmosphere in terms of the fundamental mechanical, thermodynamic and hydrodynamic laws that govern it. Ideally, once accurately defined in those terms, they can then use their formulas to predict the future state of the atmosphere. After Espy and Ferrel, introduced meteorological theory, atmospheric researchers began increasingly to apply the universal physical principles, unveiled by Newton, Boyle, Dalton, Gay Lussac and others in the 17th and 18th century, to explain the enigmatic, and erratic, behavior displayed by cyclones.

By mid-nineteenth century, Europeans and Americans had established a greatly improved weather observation network. Accordingly, atmospheric scientists could conduct more sophisticated atmospheric studies in terms of the physical laws of motion and the basic laws of thermodynamics developed during the 1840s and 1850s. This branch of meteorology, called dynamic or theoretical meteorology, evolved into a strictly scientific discipline that required a comprehensive knowledge of physics, chemistry and advanced mathematics.

Professional societies began to emerge during the 1860s. Atmospheric researchers held meetings, published journals in which they discussed new developments in atmospheric theory, and translated foreign research papers. These new channels of communication generated an awareness of current meteorological (and related) research within the community. They expanded and refined data gathering procedures and, in time, produced a substantial body of common knowledge available to all investigators. This vital step released the investigator from performing his or her own research on concepts already established, thus unifying and accelerating investigative procedures.

Eventually, the operational or synoptic meteorologist could no longer easily follow advances made in the dynamic sector. Still, the synoptic approach continued to prove indispensable as an investigative tool.

THE SYNOPTIC CHART SEES ALL, TELLS ALL

Army generals in the field need maps whereby they can display the current location and strength of their forces and, as far as known, those of the enemy as well. Such maps quickly and visually summarize the situation at hand. Meteorologists employ similar maps (which they call synoptic charts) whereupon plots of simultaneously observed atmospheric data can display a wide variety of meteorological information. With a carefully drawn synoptic chart, illustrating aerial distributions of pressure, temperature, wind and precipitation, a researcher or forecaster can easily follow the various processes associated with storm development and movement.

Elias Loomis believed that a diligent statistical investigation of atmospheric processes and detailed study of individual storms would soon reveal the laws that govern storm development. Accordingly, using synoptic charts and a variety of tables, graphs and empirical rules, he made a painstakingly study of some 150 mid-latitude storms over a period of 50 years. During the decade of the 1870s, Loomis -- and his European colleagues, Alexander Buchan and Henrick Mohn (and later Clement Ley and Max Margules) -- arrived at a consensus theory of storm development and movement.

Developing storms have a field of warm, moist air in the forward portion of an advancing cyclone with cold, dry air encroaching from the west. The denser cold air undercuts the warm air, forcing it to rise. The subsequent condensation of water vapor and release of latent heat causes the pressure to lower in the forward regions of the storm. Diverging air currents in the westerly flow aloft provide an outdraft to compensate for the converging air currents near the surface. This vital process maintains or increases the low pressure within the cyclone.

A continuous influx of colder, more dense air from the northwest at lower levels, compounded by the outflowing and descending air from the top of the storm, increases the pressure and represses convective motion in the rear regions of the storm.

Careful analyses of pressure fields revealed that the largest pressure falls occur in the forward portion (east) of the cyclone center, where the greatest upward vertical motion occurs. From this observation they determined that storms do not move but propagate. New low pressure centers form continuously in the region of heaviest precipitation -- ahead of the storm -- and simultaneously degenerate to the rear where cold and sinking air inhibits upward vertical motion.

MODIFICATIONS TO ESPY'S THERMAL THEORY

Espy became the first scientist to apply physical law to explain meteorological phenomena. In his theory, the latent heat released by a mass of air, lifted by some fortuitous means, produced all the kinetic energy displayed by the accelerating winds within vortical storms and provided the motive power to fuel cyclone development.

His quite plausible "thermal" theory appeared, at the time, to explain all the important activities observed in developing storms -- and eclipsed the current theories of Redfield and Dove. Subsequent research, however, soon revealed features in cyclonic storms that Espy's postulate could not explain. Further investigation would show that developing storms contain elements of all the then current, supposedly conflicting, theories.

Ferrel, Americas leading atmospheric investigator during the late 1800s, championed Espy's convective or thermal theory of storms. He also recognized the importance of synoptic weather analysis as practiced by Loomis and his European colleagues. Merging Loomis' graphical data with the developing field of dynamic (theoretical) meteorology, Ferell added several important modifications to Espy's thermal theory including a deflecting force caused by the earth's rotation.

Objects in free flight across the earth's surface submit to a mysterious force caused by the earth's rotation. While an object may move in a straight line, the rotation of the earth beneath the object causes it to curve to the right of its initial direction over the earth's surface. This effect, called the "Coriolis force" or, sometimes, the "deflecting force of the earth's rotation," applies to moving air as well as solid forms. (See Appendix A).

Ferrel's mathematical treatment of this strange force explained why winds converging toward a storm center acquire an anti-clockwise spiral. As high pressure forces air inward toward the low center, the earth's rotation deflects it toward the right. If not for a third force, friction between moving air and the earth's surface, the two forces would balance. The inflowing air would eventually travel in concentric circles about the low pressure center and prevent further strengthening. Friction, however, reduces the wind speed, and thus the rightward deflecting force, allowing the air to spiral gradually inward.

The Coriolis force explained away one major criticism of Espy's cyclone model. Observers had long noted that heavy rain commonly falls near the equator but does not produce the great pressure falls and cyclonic storms that occur in mid-latitude storms. Accordingly, Espy's concept of low pressure caused by condensation of water vapor became suspect.

Ferrel noted that the deflecting force that produces and maintains the gyratory motion of large-scale cyclones decreases with latitude. Thus, even though pressure may fall over areas of heavy rain in the tropics, no large-scale cyclones can develop because the deflecting force vanishes near the equator.

Hurricanes -- super-cyclones -- usually form at least ten degrees from the equator.

The Espy-Ferrel weather model evolved along theoretical and empirical lines of investigation and incorporated most of the then current meteorological theory.

THERMODYNAMIC AND HYDRODYNAMIC LAW

Verbal descriptions of natural phenomena, no matter how detailed, cannot adequately describe their origin, explain their existence or predict their future. Only mathematics, the language of the physical world, provides the means to uniquely describe a physical phenomena -- to isolate it and hold it immobile for careful inspection. This holds especially true in meteorology, where researchers deal with erratic and transitory events occurring within a large invisible and volatile medium.

However effervescent, the atmosphere must conform to the universal physical laws of nature. The laws that apply to motions within the free atmosphere come from Newton's second law of motion and from the fields of thermodynamics and hydrodynamics.

The first law of thermodynamics defines the state of a gas in terms of its pressure, temperature and density. It also defines the correspondence between heat and mechanical energy and states that the sum of the internal heat and energy within a closed system remains constant. Thus, heat may generate energy, either kinetic or potential; kinetic energy may generate heat; potential energy can metamorphose into kinetic energy and vice versa -- but nothing in a closed system can *create* energy.

Newton developed his laws initially to describe the mechanical movements of celestial bodies but they have proven to have universal application. However, to describe atmospheric motions in the objective, mathematical terms of physical law, the dynamic meteorologist must modify Newton's second law -- and the laws of thermodynamics and hydrodynamics -- to apply to a gaseous fluid (the atmosphere) flowing over a spinning sphere (the earth).

The merge of thermodynamics and the newly developed concepts of energy and mass conservation, combined with Newton's second law, allowed researchers to calculate the energy involved in storm directly from the temperature field. Thermodynamic analyses of storms revealed that, in fact, the kinetic energy observed in cyclonic vortices vastly exceeds that available through merely the release of latent heat in vertical thermals.

Localized heating, and subsequent vertical motion, could provide the initial motive power of developing cyclones, but could not account for the sustained vertical motion that occurs in mature moving cyclones. Accordingly, atmospheric investigators began to search for other processes leading to continuous large-scale vertical motion.

By late 19th century, meteorologists had advanced a number of new theories to explain cyclonic storm generation. They had yet to determine, however, why warm and cold masses of air moved about and mixed as they did. To foretell where, when or why events leading to cyclogenesis occur required a more extensive knowledge of air motions in the higher reaches of the atmosphere -- and a more comprehensive data base.

INSTABILITY AND VERTICAL MOTION

Gravity has compressed and stratified the atmosphere into layers of pressure that decrease with height. Imagine that you could isolate and make visible a layer of constant pressure some distance above the earth. Color it a diaphanous pale blue and you would see an undulating field, not unlike an ocean surface.

Up to the tropopause, temperature also decreases with height -- not exponentially but at a more-or-less steady rate. Imagine, this time, that you can visualize several pale pink layers of temperature.

In an undisturbed atmosphere the temperature and pressure surfaces would lie parallel to the earth's surface and to each other. Density of air equals the mass or weight of the air for any given volume. The volume, and therefore the density, depends on the temperature. Consequently, layers of constant density would also lie parallel to the pressure and temperature surfaces. Nowhere would a plane of temperature contact or intersect a pressure plane or a density plane and the atmosphere would settle into a state of complete (hydrostatic) equilibrium. Meteorologists call this a barotropic atmosphere.

The atmosphere, of course, never conforms to this ideal pattern. The sun heats the equator more than the poles so a layer of constant temperature would slope gently downward from the equator toward the poles. Since the excess heat at the equator expands the air while the chill of the polar regions causes it to compress, planes of constant pressure also slope downwards toward the poles. The pink constant temperature layers usually intersect the blue constant pressure layers which produces a condition meteorologists call baroclinicity -- or a lack of barotropicity.

In a baroclinic atmosphere, planes of constant temperature intersecting planes of constant pressure form long quadrilateral tubes (called solenoids) in the atmosphere. The sharper the tilt of temperature planes to pressure planes the greater the number of solenoids produced over a given region. This solenoid density, easily discerned in vertical profiles of the atmosphere, provides a measure of the instability (and thus of available potential energy) of the atmosphere.

Whenever the atmospheric circulation moves cold air into regions of warmer air, the tilt of constant temperature planes in the colder air increases with respect to the pressure field. This produces a dense field of solenoids and the atmosphere acquires increased baroclinicity. As it tries to restore equilibrium, it begins to churn thus converting potential energy to kinetic energy.

THE UPPER-AIR CONNECTION

During the late 19th century, synoptic studies continued to support the concept that a confluence of different air masses occurs during storm development. A cold air mass slides under and lifts a warmer air mass, causing condensation and latent heat release which initiates cyclonic development. At the same time, observations of cloud movements indicated a more-or-less direct connection between events occurring at the surface and the flow of air at higher levels.

During the 1860s and 70s, the Reverend William Clement Ley, of Bristol, England, made daily cloud observations for a ten-year period. His analysis of over 600 cloud observations at various levels indicated a smooth transition of cyclonic motion from the surface to the upper atmosphere. Surprisingly, however, the vertical axis of cyclones tilted backward toward the west. Meteorologists had previously assumed that, because cirrus clouds always preceded the arrival of the cyclone, surface friction slowed the lower part of the storm and the axis of cyclones accordingly tilted eastward.

Earlier investigators knew that a surface low pressure system, with low level convergence and ascending motion, requires a divergent flow at some higher level to exhaust the inflowing air. The cyclonic circulation at higher levels displaced some 300 miles west of the surface center meant that anticyclonic, and therefore divergent, flow could, and does, occur directly over the low-level cyclone. The westward tilt of cyclones confirmed the direct connection between surface storms and the general westerly circulation.

Once the link between the surface and the upper air became obvious, researchers began to expand their pursuit for vital upper-air data. In this vein, the United States and several European nations organized an International Cloud Year. During this "year", which ran from May, 1896, to July, 1897, observers logged daily motions of clouds at all possible levels. In the United States, cloud observations from 16 uniformly spaced observatories east of the Rocky Mountains filled an 800-page document that contained some 30,000 entries.

A U.S. Weather Bureau professor, Frank Bigelow, painstakingly organized and analyzed the cloud observations and recorded the movements of each cyclone and anticyclone for six levels between the surface and 30,000 feet.

He determined that surface cyclones and anticyclones persist vertically through at least 30,000 feet. Moreover, at levels above 15,000 feet, they seem embedded in a broad undulating westerly flow -- further evidence that surface cyclones and anticyclones exist as an integral part of the upper mid-latitude circulation.

Bigelow verified that, southward of the center, from the surface to about 13,000 feet, a mass of cold air tends to under cut the warm air mass. Northward of the center, the warm mass tends to overflow the cold mass, curling around towards the west as it ascends from the surface to the upper levels. This mechanical uplifting of warm, moist air contributes materially to the release of latent heat and the generation of kinetic energy necessary to initiate storms.

As knowledge of the upper atmosphere gradually accumulated, researchers determined that the undulating waves in the westerly flow contain regions of divergence ahead and convergence to the rear of upper level troughs. They further learned that a divergent flow aloft permits and enhances -- and possibly initiates -- cyclonic development while convergent flow aloft suppresses upward vertical motion and generates fair weather.

The revelation that dynamic processes in the upper troposphere influence the formation and maintenance of cyclones and anticyclones concentrated meteorological research increasingly toward the upper reaches of the atmosphere.

A MOST SURPRISING DISCOVERY

The means to measure the atmosphere, especially at higher altitudes, has always lagged well behind the needs of both the operational and the research meteorologist. Dedicated and ingenuous (to say nothing of courageous and adventuresome) investigators and scientists of the late 19th and early 20th century expended no little effort to gather upper-air data so vital to the understanding of atmospheric processes that form and guide weather systems.

The earliest upper-air measurements, excepting those taken on mountains, came from thermometers attached to the tails of kites and lofted a few hundred feet into the sky. For several decades in the middle and late 19th century, kites remained the only vehicle capable of observing conditions in the free atmosphere.

In the late 1800s, free balloon ascents began to carry men and their instruments to greater heights. Although they could ascend to incredibly high altitudes, the balloon proved both a costly and dangerous procedure for gathering data. Several French aeronauts died as their untethered balloons rose into the thin, cold air above 25,000 feet.

In 1892 a French aeronaut named Gustave Hermite placed a barometer aboard an unmanned, hydrogen-filled balloon. This new approach to upper-air observation attracted the attention of Teisserenc de Bort, a dedicated amateur meteorologist. He founded a private observatory on his own farm where he spent several years probing the upper air with instruments carried aloft by kites and balloons.

Teisserenc de Bort developed a sophisticated instrument package and an ingenious system of balloons by which to launch and recover the instruments. He used two varnished paper balloons; one small one containing just enough hydrogen to float the instrument package and a larger one that lifted the apparatus. As the balloons ascended the hydrogen expanded until, at a pre-designed altitude, the larger balloon would burst. The weight of the larger balloon's remains, added to that of the instrument package, would slowly drag the smaller balloon back to earth.

T. de Bort and his assistant tracked the balloons from two different locations with surveyor's telescopes. These instruments (called theodolites) measure both vertical and horizontal angles which provided the wind speed and direction at various heights. The angles also gave de Bort some guidance in locating the instrument package once it returned to earth.

Before de Bort, scientists generally assumed that atmospheric temperature decreased indefinitely with height. When measurements taken during balloon flights indicated otherwise they ascribed them to faulty instruments. However, de Bort's data, gathered from 236 balloon flights to altitudes between 30,000 to 45,000 feet, showed conclusively that the temperature stops decreasing with altitude somewhere near 35,000 feet.

This newfound component of the atmosphere, which de Bort called the tropopause (using Greek words that mean "sphere of change"), marks the top of the troposphere. From the surface to the tropopause, temperature decreases steadily with height. In the region above -- the stratosphere -- the temperature increases with height. In between, in the tropopause layer, temperatures remain more or less constant (isothermal).

THE WEATHER SPHERE

As Blaise Pascal demonstrated when he had his brother-in-law walk up a mountain side with a barometer, atmospheric pressure decreases with elevation. At 18 to 20 miles above the earth's surface atmospheric pressure drops to less that one percent of that at sea level. At "the top" of the atmosphere -- somewhere near 18 thousand miles above the earth's surface in the region called the exosphere -- air particles move in free orbits, subject only to the earth's gravitation and indistinguishable from other particles that orbit the earth in inter-planetary space.

Earth's gravity holds fully three-quarters of our atmosphere within the lowest 30 to 40 thousand feet -- the tropopause level below which commercial jet aircraft fly. Vertical temperature decreases at a more or less steady rate of about 5.4°F per 1000 feet through this layer. Above this level lies the stratosphere, a quiet layer of gently subsiding air that extends upward for 30 miles or so, where temperature increases with height.

Little mixing occurs between the two layers so only traces of water vapor and polluting aerosols from the troposphere find their way into the stratosphere. Important things happen in the stratosphere but the weather that most concerns us in our daily lives occurs in the lowest 20 to 30 thousand feet of the atmosphere.

In general, weather develops from upward vertical motion produced by warmer air in lower regions rising through cooler air in upper regions. At the isothermal (tropopause) level, buoyant parcels of air reach a level of environmental compatibility and stop rising. The sinking air from the stratosphere prevents penetration by all but the strongest upward moving currents. Thus the troposphere, sometimes called the weather sphere, contains virtually all of Earth's weather. de Bort had found the ceiling to the world's weather.

APPENDIX A

CYCLONES, CAROUSELS AND CORIOLIS

Ferrel formally introduced the Coriolis force, sometimes called the "deflecting force of the earth's rotation," into meteorological science. Objects in free flight across the earth's surface, be they artillery shells, airplanes or atmospheric currents, succumb to a strange force caused by the earth's rotation. Such objects move in straight lines and would so appear to an observer in space. As the earth spins from west to east beneath them, however, they appear to an earth-bound observer to curve to the right of their direction of movement.

The earth turns from west to east on its axis of rotation, tilted slightly away from its plane of orbit around the sun. Each day, any particular point on the earth's surface describes a circular path on a plane perpendicular to the earth's axis of rotation. The distance the point moves in one day equals $2\pi R$, the circumference of the circle of rotation, where R is the perpendicular distance from the earth's axis to the point on the earth's surface. R varies with latitude from about 4000 miles at the equator to zero at the poles. Thus, the angular speed of a point on earth depends on its latitude and varies from essentially zero at the poles to about 1000 miles per hour at the equator.

A platform rotating constantly from left to right, (a carousel in the amusement park for instance) could serve to demonstrate the disconcerting effect of the Coriolis force. The angular speed of a whirling disk (a carousel) decreases with distance from its outer edge, approaching zero at the center.

A ball rolled gently by a rider from the outer edge of the carousel toward its center will turn to the right rather than follow a straight line across the platform. The ball has an initial speed toward the right equal to the angular speed of the edge of the platform. The ball retains this speed as it moves toward the center. The angular speed of the platform over which it moves, however, decreases steadily with distance toward the center. Thus, the ball gains angular speed with respect to the platform surface as it moves toward the center and, rather than moving in a straight line toward the center, deviates to the right.

Conversely, a ball launched from the center of the platform toward the edge would have an initial angular speed -- from right to left -- equal to the center of the platform. Since the angular speed of the platform increases progressively with distance from the center, the ball moves with progressively less speed than the platform, causing it to deviate (again) to the right of its initial path.

A ball placed at the middle of the platform would immediately gain an angular speed equal to that point of the platform. It would then tend, according to Newton's first law, to remain at rest, with respect to the platform, unless acted upon by an external force. In this case, the centrifugal force of the rotating platform would deflect the ball toward the edge. As it moved outward, the ball would move with progressively less speed than the platform and would deviate (again) toward the right.

Parcels of air moving over the earth's surface also yield to this phenomenon. When low pressure develops in a cyclone, higher surrounding pressure begins to push air into the center. The Coriolis force generated by the earth's rotation, bends the flow to the right. At the same time, surface friction slows the inward flow which reduces the Coriolis force. The combined forces of pressure, friction and the Coriolis effect causes air to gently spiral inward toward the low pressure center.

CHAPTER TEN

INTO THE 20TH CENTURY

**Wherein we unfold the history of early 20th century atmospheric
scientists as they advance the theoretical knowledge of meteorology by
applying the physical laws and theory developed in the 19th century. We
chronicle meteorology's second revolution following World War II
wherein atmospheric scientists utilize computers and other new instruments along with the increased frequency and accuracy of upper air
observation to advance theoretical meteorology and improve forecast
accuracy.**

"The wave or polar front theory of cyclones was a most significant and
far-reaching contribution toward describing, on the basis of sound dynamic
and energetic reasoning, the observed three-dimensional structure of the
cyclone, its evolution in time, and its role in the general circulation of the
atmosphere. Developed under the leadership of V. Bjerknes, it represents an
outstanding example of synthesis in meteorological theory, introducing novel
ideas and, at the same time, incorporating and substantiating many of the
results of 19th century and early 20th century cyclone theory."
        -- Gisela Kutzbach

BRIDGING THE GAP

Over the decades, synoptic meteorologists, using statistics, charts and graphs made significant contributions to meteorological science. The dynamic meteorologist, using deductive methods of research, advanced the theoretical understanding of the atmosphere, and the turbulent features within it, in terms of the basic physical laws of nature.

Each approach has proved indispensable to the other. The analytical studies furnished a data base the researcher could use to test his results, and provided the foundation for further theoretical research. In return, theoretical analyses often provided empirical researchers with new insight for deeper investigation.

The late 1800s saw several gifted scientists from the United States and Europe enter the field of meteorological research. Alexander Buchan from Scotland, William Thompson (Lord Kelvin) from England, Theodor Reye, Hermann Helmholtz and Henrik Mohn from Germany and H. Peslin from France, working concurrently with Ferrel, Loomis and Bigelow of the United States all made meaningful contributions to the thermal theory of cyclones and to the practical application of meteorological science.

THE TROPOPAUSE -- THE WEATHER CEILING

In the late 1800s and early 1900s, some knowledge of the upper air had been gained from cloud motions, mountain observations, occasional balloon and kite soundings and from manned balloon ascents.

Tesserenc de Bort's discovery of the upper inversion that marks the tropopause prompted new avenues of research which soon revealed several significant relationships between the tropopause and other, lower level, meteorological processes.

William Henry Dines, in a detailed study of about 200 upper-air observations, found a positive relationship between surface pressure, the height of the tropopause, and the average temperature between the surface and the tropopause. He noted that the tropopause lifted during the summer months and lowered during winter months. He also noted that the tropopause lowered over surface cyclonic circulations. This indicated a thinner, cold atmosphere beneath the tropopause which explained the lower surface pressure in cyclones. Conversely, he noted that the tropopause rises above a warm anticyclone. A thick tropospheric layer over anticyclones accounted for the higher surface pressure.

These observations led Dines to conclude that processes in upper troposphere and the lower stratosphere contributed more to surface cyclonic circulation than the thermal processes in the troposphere postulated by Espy.

THE POLAR FRONT/AIR MASS THEORY

Air residing over a given region of the world gradually acquires the characteristics of its climate (e.g. polar, tropical maritime). During the atmosphere's more quiet periods, the upper air currents smooth out into large, gently flowing waves of relatively small amplitude. At the surface, large bodies of air may stagnate over a given region for several days or even weeks.

The many climates of the world generate masses of air with very different combinations of temperature and moisture content. In the simplest case, the differential heating of the earth by the sun causes cold air to pool in the polar regions while large masses of warm air bask over the warm tropical oceans. Somewhere in the mid-latitudes there lies a zone of sharply contrasting temperature and humidity -- called a discontinuity -- that separates the two air masses.

The discontinuity lies in a weak trough of low pressure between the cold anticyclone to the north and the warm anticyclone to the south. North of the zone the wind flows from the east and south of the zone it flows from the west, producing a cyclonic wind shear across the discontinuity.

The two air masses lie in a state of uneasy juxtaposition and any small disturbance in the atmospheric flow can cause a small protuberance (wave) to appear. Under certain conditions, the wind shift (cyclonic) across the zone, coupled with vertical motion caused by rising warm air on the south side and sinking cold air on the north side, could initiate a wave.

During the first World War a team of meteorologists, under the direction of Velhelm and Jakob Bjerknes at the Bergen School of Meteorology in Norway, employed this concept -- a discontinuity between polar and tropical air masses -- to create a simple and essentially correct description of storm development.

In their scheme, a zone of discontinuity (which they called the polar front) separates tropical and polar air masses. Owing to some instability on the polar front, a wave develops and moves along the frontal boundary. The colder drier air from the north wedges under the warmer, more moist and less dense tropical air, forcing it to rise. As the warm air rises, water vapor condenses into liquid water droplets and releases its latent heat. The potential energy released during the rearrangement of the different air masses and the release of latent heat provides the kinetic energy for continued cyclogenesis.

The underlying concept of the Bjerknes Polar Front/Air Mass storm model obviously rested upon extensive investigations carried out during the previous century. The genius of the model lies in the synthesis of disparate segments of knowledge into a lucid and comprehensive view of intricate atmospheric processes. With but few modifications, the Bjerknes cyclone model, became -- and remains -- an invaluable tool for the forecaster and a focal point for subsequent atmospheric research.

OBSERVING THE ATMOSPHERE

In the early 1900s, the Weather Bureau used untethered "pilot" balloons (called "pibals") to determine wind direction and speed. A balloon inflated with helium will rise a known distance each minute, depending on the weight of the balloon and the amount of helium used.

To achieve a known rate of ascent, the observer fills the balloon with helium until the balloon lifts a standard weight. The observer tracks the balloon with a surveying instrument (a theotolite). Using the known ascent rate the height of the balloon, he calculates the height each minute. Then, from changes in the direction and the increase in the vertical angle, the observer can trigonometricly determine the balloons drift during the last minute -- and translate the figures into wind speed and direction.

Using this technique, observers could determine the wind speed and direction up to about 10,000 feet in fair weather. Pibals, however, have limitations. They can measure only the lower wind during stormy periods because of cloud cover and, even in fair weather, strong winds sometimes quickly sweep the balloon out of sight.

For a time after World War I, weather services used airplanes to gather upper-air temperature, pressure and moisture data. In the late 1930s, aircraft deployed at various locations made as many as 30 "soundings" of the atmosphere each day -- reaching to 16,000 feet on occasion. As with pibals, however, airplanes could not make observations during stormy weather. Moreover, airplanes proved a dangerous and expensive means to gather data.

In 1927, two Frenchmen patched together a crude but effective instrument package that could measure pressure, temperature and humidity during balloon ascents and radio the information back to earth. Radio direction finders could track the balloon and thus determine the wind flow to very high altitudes regardless of weather conditions.

The invention and deployment of this device (called the radiosonde) provided at last a means to cheaply and safely measure the important features of the upper atmosphere. Just before the start of World War II, the United States installed radiosonde observatories at all Weather Bureau and military aircraft stations.

Post-war technology has produced a stream of marvelous new instruments for observing upper-air conditions. Rockets can obtain data up to altitudes of about 200,000 feet, heights unreachable by balloons. Both Doppler radar and "bedspring" radar profilers can detect and follow tiny differences in air density that provides turbulence data and changes in wind speed through layers of the atmosphere. Weather satellites, in addition to viewing entire storm systems, indeed several storm systems, can sense the state of the ocean and measure (approximately) the vertical temperature and humidity profile of the atmosphere and the surface winds. The radiosonde, however, remains the reliable standby and provides the standard against which new systems are tested.

MODIFICATIONS TO THE BJERKNES MODEL

Between the two world wars, increased data from radiosonde networks improved immensely the knowledge of the atmosphere structure. Simultaneous measurements, obtained from swarms of balloon-borne instruments, permitted researchers to construct a "snapshot" of large-scale weather patterns, including wind direction and speed, temperature, pressure and moisture at various heights.

Owing to a lack of upper-air data, Bjerknes and his colleagues had necessarily overemphasized processes occurring at and near the earth's surface. When the radiosonde began to return a generous amount of reliable upper-air data, Bjerknes and his colleague, Jorgen Holmboe, added an essential feature to the Norwegian cyclone model. Their post-war studies revealed that certain configurations of the upper level circulation could initiate the low-level vertical motions that researchers usually attributed to thermal convection.

As observed earlier by Ley and Bigelow, the more-or-less circular closed low and high pressure areas at the surface gradually change into a series of open waves at higher altitudes. Moreover, the trough of each wave contains a region of convergence to the rear of the lowest pressure region and divergence ahead of it.

Bjerknes and Holmboe found that zones of divergence in upper-air waves frequently cause upward vertical motion and pressure changes within potentially unstable surface air. Air flowing into a region of lowering pressure generates a wave on the polar front. Cold air flowing into the incipient storm from the west mechanically lifts warmer, moist air east of the center. As the rising air cools to the point of condensation, it releases latent heat. This creates or enhances temperature differences between the rising air and the environment, adding buoyancy to the rising air and producing an additional, dynamic, lifting force. If not for the addition of dynamic lifting produced by the release of latent heat, vertical motions within storms would cease at a much lower level than they commonly do.

The combination of dynamical and mechanical lifting of the surface air creates horizontal temperature differences which, in turn, create solenoids or baroclinicity -- a source of considerable potential energy. Upon conversion, the potential energy provides the kinetic energy necessary to overcome the frictional forces and accelerate the winds within a storm.

The deepening low then creates stronger temperature contrasts leading to further development. Not until cold air wraps around the low pressure center does the upward vertical motion cease and the storm begin to decay.

Thus, while recognizing the importance of surface heating in the development of vertical motions, release of latent heat and cyclogenesis, Bjerknes and Homboe showed that divergence and baroclinic instability within the broad upper-level westerlies not only play an important role in the development of cyclones, but actually initiate low-level thermodynamic processes that generate cyclonic storms.

In 1937, Jacob Bjkernes demonstrated that the slow-moving or stationary long waves in the upper atmosphere circled the globe. Two years later, Carl Rossby, a disciple of Vilhelm Bjkernes, developed a mathematical equation to predict the movement of the hemispheric westerly waves and meteorology became global rather than regional.

THE METEOROLOGIST AT WAR

Frequently, either by design or accident, weather proves a key element in battle. During World War II, where the airplane often decided the outcome of battles and campaigns, weather and the meteorologist who forecasted it became a vital component in practically every phase of the conflict.

The war demanded full mobilization and soon after Pearl Harbor the Weather Bureau became officially engaged in the war. In addition to providing some 700 meteorologists for military operations, Weather Bureau employees gave crash courses in weather science to military personnel. By the end of the conflict, the military's Air Weather Service operated over 900 weather stations employing over 19,000 men. The Navy's Aerological Service grew from under 700 people in 1941 to over 6000 by war's end.

Some meteorologists operated from relatively safe positions behind the lines but many engaged the war at first hand. Uniformed weather men went in with the first waves during invasions of Africa, Europe and dozens of Pacific atolls. Others flew reconnaissance flights to determine what weather conditions our bombers would encounter during raids over Europe and Japanese occupied territory.

As World War II began, despite recent advances in cyclogenetic theory, operational meteorologists still only dimly understood the three-dimensional structure of low-pressure areas. Outmoded concepts of the general atmospheric circulation prevailed in the applied field of forecasting. Despite compelling new theoretical revelations, forecasting remained an empirical art that employed but little of the rapidly advancing field of thermodynamics.

By the close of World War II, aided enormously by the newly established and expanded radiosonde network and war-time research, investigators had pieced together a much clearer picture of the upper-air flow patterns. Armed with new concepts of atmospheric structure and behavior, the world's weather services returned their attention to the common task of understanding and forecasting the weather.

Emerging from the ashes of the war and feeding on the subsequent political unrest, the pace of scientific discovery and technological innovation exceeded the expectations of even the most visionary futurist. Technologists, capitalizing on the flood of new knowledge, have generated ever more sophisticated tools and machinery with which to probe the mysteries of the atmosphere. The meteorological community has kept pace with the spectacular advances in techno-science -- and in some cases have led the field. Atmospheric scientists have amassed more knowledge in the few decades since the end of WW II than during the entire history leading to that point.

CHAPTER ELEVEN

THE NEW METEOROLOGY

Wherein we continue to unfold the history of weather as atmospheric scientists of the mid-20th century further advance the theoretical knowledge of meteorology. We chronicle meteorology's second revolution following World War II wherein atmospheric scientists utilize new instruments along with the increased frequency and accuracy of upper air observations to advance theoretical meteorology and improve forecast accuracy. Additionally, we recount the marriage of meteorological theory with the computer, an experiment that ultimately produced weather forecasts of timeliness and accuracy that far exceeds those produced by humans.

"By the summer of 1952, there was mounting evidence that the crudest of numerical methods was capable of attaining an average accuracy comparable with that of forecasts prepared by conventional methods."
-- Philip Duncan Thompson

A NEW ATTITUDE

The America that emerged victorious from the second World War bore little resemblance to the one that reluctantly entered it several years earlier. Victory on the world's battlefields produced a sense of national accomplishment that banished the memories of fear, anger and bewilderment so prevalent in the era between the two world wars. America transcended its isolationist uncertainty and entered the post-war arena as the confident, dynamic leader of the free world with a manifest duty to champion global democracy.

A similar transformation occurred in the field of meteorology. New technology, developed during the war, opened new avenues of investigation and, more importantly, opened a new, expansive mode of thinking. Before the war, the U.S. Weather Bureau had stoutly resisted efforts to introduce the new concepts advanced by the Bergen school. Weather Bureau forecasters, citing the press of operational deadlines, continued to forecast from two-dimensional weather maps. Despite increasing interest by academic meteorologists, and repeated visits to the U. S. by Bergen disciples, they expressed little interest in learning the dynamics of the phenomena they forecasted.

The threat of war and an influx of foreign talent into the American universities changed all that. Just prior to and during the war, the United States universities trained hundreds of new meteorologists in the latest concepts and techniques based on the Bjerknes weather model.

A very large number of war-time meteorologists became permanently hooked on weather and remained in the field after the war. Soldier-meteorologists returning to the United States joined a cadre consisting of the greatest single pool of meteorological talent in the world. This eminent field could count among its fraternity such notable scientists as Rossby, Meisinger, Wexler, Reichelderfer, Spilhaus, Willett, Byers, Sutcliffe, Sawyer, Clapp, Namais, Haurwitz, Petterssen, Newton and Palmén, followed by Charney, Eliaison, Thompson, Smagorinski, Hoskins, Reed, Phillips, Eady, Starr, Miller and Panofsky (to mention a few). This august pool of talent launched a many-faceted assault on the vexing problems of dynamic meteorology and weather forecasting. Among their many accomplishments perhaps numerical (computer) weather forecasting stands as their greatest.

DR. FRANCIS REICHELDERFER

In large measure, the credit for transforming the U.S. Weather Bureau into a modern operation, admired and emulated the world over, belongs to a Navy pilot and aeronaut, Francis Reichelderfer. Educated as a chemist, Reichelderfer volunteered for the U.S. Naval Flying Reserve Corps in 1917.

He received three months training in meteorology at Harvard's historic Blue Hill Observatory before his flight training.

As a navy pilot, qualified for balloons, dirigibles and airplanes, Reichelderfer maintained an intense interest in meteorology. Assigned to the Naval Air Station at Hampton Roads, Virginia, he began his dual role of pilot and aviation weather forecaster. One bombing exercise, in which his flight ran into an unforecasted squall line (cold front), focused his interest on improved aviation forecasts.

In due course Reichelderfer went to Washington, D.C. where, as director of the Navy's aerological service, he installed the Bergen school principles as standard practice throughout the Navy. While in Washington, he met Carl Rossby, a product of the Bergen school then working for the Weather Bureau. The combination of Rossby and Reichelderfer would, from that moment, constitute a major force in introducing air-mass and storm-front analysis into United States weather services -- and advancing meteorological theory and weather forecasting in general.

The surge of aviation in the late 1920s generated a demand for flight-weather forecasts that overburdened the Weather bureau. Reichelderfer, citing the need for improved aviation forecasts, persuaded the Daniel Guggenheim Fund for the Promotion of Aeronautics to establish the Guggenheim Committee on Aeronautical Meteorology -- with himself as a member and Rossby as chairman.

Reichelderfer then persuaded the Guggenheim Foundation to fund a model weather service for commercial flights between Los Angeles and Oakland, California -- with Rossby in charge. Over the years, the practical success of this program would attract many theoretical researchers who wanted to gain personal experience in weather prediction.

A few years later, again under the urging of Reichelderfer, the Guggenheim Foundation funded a course in theoretical meteorology for navy aerologists at the Massachusetts Institute of Technology. Reichelderfer taught synoptic meteorology, using the Bergen school methods, naturally, and hired Rossby to teach the theoretical portion of the course. In a short time this advanced course in meteorology expanded into a fully developed Department of Meteorology with Rossby as chairman.

In 1938, Reichelderfer became Chief of the Weather Bureau. During his 25-year tenure as weather chief, he developed and presided over the most modern and effective national weather service in the world. Under his guidance the Weather Bureau embraced the latest technological and scientific advances, and transformed operational meteorology from an art form into a science.

In an era where most government agencies padded their budgets and clamored for additional funds, Reichelderfer pressed his modest but effective programs to fruition on a minimal budget and each year proudly returned to the treasury a small "surplus." Each year a grateful congress looked over his reasonable budget proposal -- and made the standard cut in his request for funds.

BEYOND BERGEN

Studies around the turn of the century, based upon very limited upper-air information, had established the vertical continuity between lower-level and upper-level flow patterns. In the 1930s and 1940s, aided by an influx of quality data from the radiosonde network, atmospheric investigators verified the dynamic link between the surface and the upper atmosphere. Even during the great war, important meteorological investigation and research continued in the universities.

With abundant upper air data, it became possible to employ a type of synoptic chart that provided a detailed vertical picture of the atmosphere. Imagine a large vertical plane slicing through the air between Houston, Texas, and Chicago, Illinois. The various horizontal (nearly) planes of temperature, pressure, density, moisture, wind speed and so on would become lines forming a vertical profile, called a cross section, of the mid-western atmosphere. On such profiles, the westward tilt of the polar front, the change in wind with height and the potential energy available from temperature differences become quite obvious.

Studies of cross sections of the atmosphere made it increasingly apparent that some developing storms draw their kinetic energy from potential energy supplies in the lower troposphere, gradually extending upward to higher levels, Most storms, however, develop under intense circulations that appear first at higher levels and transfer inertia to the lower strata.

Erik Palmén introduced three-dimensional frontal analysis to American meteorologists during his visits to Chicago from his native Finland. Although time-consuming to construct, researchers to date have found have no better tool for viewing and studying features -- and anomalies -- of the upper air.

Palmén's earlier studies had hinted at the possibility of a channel of high-speed winds near the tropopause. Radiosonde data had also suggested that strong winds existed at that level but researchers attributed the clues to instrument error. Accordingly, American airmen flying into such regions did not expect the high winds they sometimes encountered. During bombing raids on Japan, pilots occasionally found themselves literally flying backward in jet stream headwinds.

After the war, Rossby and Palmén introduced the concept of a jet stream enfolded within the meanderings of the upper westerlies. They further associated frontal and tropopause structures with the upper-level flow and noted that low-level cyclogenesis often occurs in tandem with changes in upper-level features. Jules Charney provided further evidence of this phenomena when he introduced his "baroclinic instability theory" of storm development.

OUR APPROXIMATE ATMOSPHERE

The prediction of atmospheric motion requires the integration and simultaneous solution of four equations: the equation(s) of motion, the equation of continuity, the equation of state, and the equation of energy (See Appendix A). The extraordinary complexity of the atmosphere, however, does not readily lend itself to a rigorous solution of these equations.

The composition of the atmosphere varies rapidly in space and time owing mainly to condensation and evaporation of water vapor but also to the continuous inflow and outflow of radiant heat that maintains the atmosphere in a constant state of vertical and horizontal movement.

Radiation and condensation, both of which depend upon the amount of water vapor in the air, generate a continuous exchange of heat throughout the atmosphere that causes it to remain always in motion. The motion of the atmosphere, however, continually changes the distribution of water vapor in the air -- which affects the heat exchange process.

This circular interdependence between the motion and the distribution of heat and water vapor leads to insurmountable mathematical difficulties when attempting an exact solution of the atmospheric equations of motion.

Fortunately, meteorologists have learned mathematical techniques that yield considerable knowledge about the state and dynamic behavior of the atmosphere by using systematic assumptions and approximations to real conditions.

For example, elimination of all heat terms in the equations of energy and state renders a much simpler mathematical description for the atmosphere. Although a gross simplification, the equation for such a thermally inactive atmosphere yields more readily to solution and still provides useful information about atmospheric motion.

Similarly, the assumption of a steady zonal motion, symmetric about the axis of the earth and flowing over a smooth, flat earth along the circles of latitude without any changes of state, produces satisfactory solutions to the equations of continuity, state and energy. An assumption that the intersection of planes of temperature with planes of pressure (solenoids) describes the variation of the wind and satisfies the equation of motion. Even after making all these assumptions, researchers obtain a surprisingly good first approximation to observed atmospheric motions.

In 1947, Jules Charney, published a paper, *"On the Scale of Atmospheric Motions."* In his paper he sorted out the effect that each of the various terms in the hydrodynamic and thermodynamic equations contributes to atmospheric motion. By introducing approximations for certain terms and eliminating others whose effects he deemed small or insignificant, he combined the six equations that govern the atmosphere into a single equation. Charney thus eliminated most computational difficulties inherent in solving the highly complex meteorological equations.

Charney's equation successfully predicted the structure of incipient frontal waves, giving them realistic growth rates and wavelengths. It also clearly indicated that dynamic instability in the high-level, baroclinic, westerly winds not only generates low-level storms but actually provides the primary source of energy for cyclonic storm development. Accordingly, emphasis on research quickly shifted from low-level discontinuities to dynamic processes that associate upper-level troughs and jets with low-level fronts.

Charney's paper stimulated a surge in meteorological research. Luminaries such as Rossby, V. and J. Bjerknes, Jorgen Holmboe, Eric Eady, R. C. Sutcliff and Eric Palmén, quickly followed Charney's lead, generating a flood of research papers. In a relatively short time they firmly established the connection between baroclinicity in the upper atmosphere and surface cyclogenesis. Most if not all cyclones develop from the top down.

DYNAMIC BEGINNINGS

As early as 1860 researchers had developed the several meteorological equations that describe the behavior of atmospheric flow. In 1904, V. Bjerknes stated that Newton's equations of motion combined with the Boyle-Charles-Dalton equation of state, the equation of mass continuity, and the thermodynamic energy equations provided the information necessary to predict the future state of the atmosphere.

Theoretically, given sufficient observational data, the meteorological equations could define the current state of the atmosphere and forecast the future state for given intervals of time. Cleveland Abbe, then chief scientist for the Weather Bureau, agreed. He postulated, again theoretically, that he could solve the highly complex hydrodynamic and thermodynamic equations and produce an accurate weather forecast using graphical methods.

Practically, the labor required to solve the formidable, non-linear, meteorological equations by whatever means would have to wait for the invention of the computer some years hence. Lewis Fry Richardson, a British mathematician and physicist vividly illustrated this point when, during World War I, he tried to make a numerical weather forecast.

The indefatigable Richardson drove an ambulance on the western front during the war. Between shifts he performed the many thousands of additions, subtractions and multiplications necessary to graphically solve his meteorological equations and produced, after several months, a six-hour forecast for an area about as large as Europe.

His forecast, which had storms moving at the speed of sound and traveling from east to west rather than west to east, failed spectacularly. His mistakes, however, revealed some of the pitfalls of numerical methods. With a few adjustments, his techniques proved quite suitable once electronic computers became available to reduce the time required to compute a forecast.

Even a visionary such as Richardson could not foresee the rapid development of high-speed computers that would emerge a few decades later. He did, however, fantasize a computer capable of calculating the future weather faster than it really happens. He envisioned a giant room occupied by

64,000 individual "human computers." There, using information passed rapidly by flashing colored lights, telegraph, and pneumatic tubes, they would rapidly calculate tomorrow's weather.

THE COMPUTER

While research continued within the academic arena, the synoptic or operational weather forecaster still depended mainly on personal experience to forecast storm development and movement. The first decade following World War II saw a complete and dramatic reversal of that situation. Numerical forecasting performed by high-speed computers rapidly became, first feasible, then operationally successful.

In 1946, John von Neumann organized the Electronic Computer Project at the Institute for Advanced Study (IAS) in Princeton, New Jersey and singled out weather prediction as a problem suitable for special attention. He selected Jule Charney to establish the Meteorology Group within the project specifically to find means of solving the very complex, interactive and highly non-linear problems involved with numerical weather forecasting.

By 1950, Charney had generated a successful weather forecast using the ENIAC (Electronic Numerical Integrator And Computer). It took ENIAC 24 hours to produce a 24-hour forecast. By 1952, the IAS had developed their own computer, the ancestor of all modern digital computers, that could make the same forecast in less than five minutes.

COMPUTER FORECASTS

The success of the early computer forecasts prompted the three major weather services in the United States to combine resources in a joint effort to improve operational weather forecasting using numerical methods. The Weather Bureau, the Air Force Air Weather Service and Naval Weather Service formed the Joint Numerical Weather Prediction Unit (JNWPU) in July, 1954. The group acquired an IBM 701 in March 1955, and by September began to routinely produce numerical weather forecasts for operational use.

The success of numerical weather prediction, using mathematical weather models, rests largely on correctly deciding which features to include and which to leave out. In the beginning, owing to the very limited memory of primitive computers, programmers had but few choices.

The JNWPU began operations in 1954 with the most sophisticated weather model of the day -- a three-level model developed by Charney in Princeton. Unfortunately, although theoretically valid, essential components had been left out and the model proved to have little forecasting skill. A two-level model developed by Thompson also showed little forecasting skill and the JNWPU necessarily retreated to the much simpler single-level barotropic atmospheric model with an areal distribution restricted to just North America barotropic model while they solved the problems of more advanced models.

Using but one level means that no vertical motion can occur and the model cannot convert potential energy to kinetic energy. Thus, although they can propagate waves, such models cannot forecast storm development -- a severe limit to forecasting skill.

By 1958 they had identified and solved the major difficulties and began issuing skillful, timely numerical predictions to Weather Bureau forecasters. By 1960 they had acquired a more powerful computer, the IBM 704, and were issuing products equal or surpassing those created manually by Weather Bureau forecasters. With each advance in computing power there followed more sophisticated forecast models. By 1962, the IBM 7094 computer began running a three-level baroclinic model that could predict the development of storms with considerable skill for the entire northern hemisphere.

The computer forecast, a propitious marriage of technology and theory, rapidly and dramatically improved the Weather Bureau's forecasting skill. Although for many years operational meteorologists (forecasters) continually referred to computer forecasts as "guidance" material, by the end of the 1960s the computer could make a better upper-air forecast than the meteorologist.

Over the years, breakthroughs in computer technology became the norm. The National Meteorological Center successively acquired six computers, each about six times as powerful as its predecessor. The accuracy of numerical weather forecasting also increased, although not by several orders of magnitude as did the computer.

The forecast area steadily increased from local to global using the combination of ever more powerful computers and increasingly sophisticated weather models. Most global models now contain seven or more layers, differentiate between land and sea, recognize mountains and clouds, gather moisture from the surface, precipitate it out in storms, and appropriately distribute radiant and latent heat.

ENTER CHAOS

Three-day forecasts improved steadily but longer-range forecasts refused to yield to raw computing power. In 1976, Edward Lorenz, a mathematician who became enamored with weather while serving as an Army Air Corps forecaster during World War II, discovered the reason.

Computer weather models work with a global grid that distributes some 65,000 data points about 60 miles apart. The computer fits real data from about 10,000 global observations onto the grid -- reasonably concentrated over land areas but widely scattered over oceans and deserts. The computer uses the observed data to "guess" what conditions exist at the other 55,000 points. Unfortunately, the many varying external and internal influences that drive our complex, dissipative and dynamically fluid atmosphere, complicate its motions far beyond human ability to isolate or measure. Lorenz called this fundamental instability in the atmosphere the chaotic factor. Chaos causes forecasts generated by computers to diverge, sometimes considerably, from the real weather.

Even our most careful observations only approximate the true condition of the air. Thus, the computer forecast starts with a very poor estimate of real atmospheric conditions. Small errors in the initial analysis often cause the computer to forecast weather that barely resembles that which actually occurs. The more chaotic the atmosphere at observation time, the greater the error in the forecast. According to Lorenz, these minute, practically immeasurable features constitute the inherent and inescapable chaos of the atmosphere.

Even if meteorologists could get accurate data at points one foot apart over the entire earth, small fluctuations in the air between data points still would introduce tiny perturbations that would swiftly grow. As a result, atmospheric conditions would sooner or later deviate from those forecast by the computer.

THE BUTTERFLY EFFECT

To illustrate this long-term consequence of small atmospheric motions, Lorenz whimsically likened it to the effect of a butterfly which, by flapping its wings in Brazil, could eventually affect the sizes and paths of large storms around the world.

The future of long-range forecasts depends on maneuvering around the so-called 'Butterfly Effect'. Currently, National Weather Center forecasters, awaiting mathematical solutions to the dilemma, employ a technique that actually uses the chaotic effect. They make several forecasts, each with slightly different initial conditions. When all the forecasts agree, meteorologists assume a low chaos factor and issue their predictions with confidence. When few or none agree, they issue their forecasts with much lower confidence.

The Butterfly Effect makes long-range forecasting difficult. Yet we depend on chaos for variability. If small perturbations in the atmosphere did not increase and cascade, the world's weather would stall, or move with the monotonous regularity of a ticking clock and we would lose the excitement of watching our next weather experience unfold.

The chaotic effect uncovered by Lorenz certainly did not solve all weather forecasting problems, but it did provide an essential explanation of a wide range of other phenomena. In a sense, Lorenz made a dual discovery -- chaotic behavior of physical systems on one scale, and the notion that an underlying sense of order dictates seemingly chaotic behavior.

APPENDIX A

SOME DEFINITIONS

The equations of motion: A set of (three) hydrodynamical equations representing the application of Newton's second law of motion to a fluid (atmospheric) system. The total acceleration of an individual fluid particle is equated to the sum of the forces acting on the particle within the fluid.

The equation of continuity: A hydrodynamic equation which expresses the principle of conservation of mass in a fluid (or the atmosphere).

The equation of state: An equation relating temperature, pressure, and volume of a system in thermodynamic equilibrium.

Hydrostatic approximation: The assumption that the atmosphere is in hydrostatic equilibrium.

Hydrostatic equilibrium: The state of a fluid (the atmosphere in this case) whose surfaces of constant pressure and constant mass (or density) coincide and are horizontal throughout. Complete balance exists between the force of gravity and the pressure force. The relation between the pressure and the geometric height is given by the hydrostatic equation. Under hydrostatic equilibrium, the internal energy of an atmospheric column bears a fixed ratio to the potential energy of the column. Consequently, both forms are frequently combined, the sum being called the *total potential energy.*

Geostrophic wind: an approximation to the real wind that assumes the Coriolis acceleration exactly balances the pressure force.

Geostrophic approximation: The assumption that the geostrophic wind can replace the horizontal wind for computational purposes without significant error.

Hydrostatic equation: A simplified version of the equations of motion that related the change of pressure with height to the product of its density and the force of gravity.

CHAPTER TWELVE

THE HISTORY OF CLIMATE

Wherein we chronicle the climate of earth over the eons as it changes with the development and drift of the continents, the rise of huge mountain chains and variations in solar radiance. We further note the development of weather lore by primitive Man, the first form of climatology, and its subsequent refinement over the ages, and outline our recent concern over climate changes caused by modern industrial pollution.

"Climate is not a constant thing. It has always changed and it will always change."
-- Jack Williams

THE EVOLUTION OF CLIMATE

Paleontologists have determined that the oldest rocks on earth date back about 4.2 billion years. Since that time, throughout Earth's history, major changes in climate, associated with continental drift, shifting seas and mountain building, have repeatedly and profoundly affected existing life forms.

From the characteristics and composition of rocks formed over the eons, geologists and archeologists have discovered and dated (approximately) a number of climacteric biological, geological and climatological events. Of many momentous events in Earth's history, these stand out as highly significant; the appearance of life at about 3.8 billion years ago; the Proterozoic-Cambrian demarcation which saw the rise of invertebrates and a marked increase in atmospheric oxygen; the Permian-Triassic demarkation when the super-continent of Pangea fragmented; the Cretaceous-Tertiary transition that featured the great extinction of dinosaurs and the rise of primates; the great Pleistocene cooling, dated at about 2 million years ago; and the beginning of our own Holocene interglacial climate that includes the last few thousand years of recorded human history.

The Cretaceous-Tertiary divide marks the beginning of the Cenozoic Era and the beginning of the "Cenozoic decline," a gradual cooling of the earth leading to the great glaciations of the Pleistocene ice age -- an age in which we still live. The cooling began slowly about 65 million years ago. Around 40 million years ago the temperature dropped abruptly and sea ice began to form around Antarctica. Around 27 million years ago another rapid cooling caused glaciers to appear on the Antarctic continent. By 10 million years ago sheets of ice covered Antarctica and mountain glaciers had appeared in the northern hemisphere. Two million years ago sheets of ice began to form in the northern hemisphere.

Since the beginning of the Pleistocene, two million years ago, the quantity of glacial ice on earth has fluctuated on a more-or-less regular basis -- expanding and contracting in cycles of approximately 100,000 years..

We currently live in one of the interglacial periods, called the Holocene. During such warm, relatively benign respites from cold and ice, plants and animals generally thrive but significant climate anomalies still happen. "The Climatic Optimum," a very warm period, occurred between about 5000 and 4000 B.C. Between 1450 A.D. to 1850 A.D., a cold period (appropriately called "The Little Ice Age") caused a growth in glaciation that reached near ice-age proportions.

Excepting these two anomolies, Earth's climate has remained remarkably constant since we entered the Holocene some 10,000 years ago. But, even in "normal" times, drought and flood bring suffering and grief to many. Small wonder that humans from the earliest times have fretted over the weather and tried to divine its intentions.

CLIMATE AND STATISTICS

We expect the weather to capriciously exhibit all forms of inconvenient behavior as it cycles through daily, weekly, and seasonal time periods. However, we also count on it to behave within certain bounds -- to depart only incrementally, and then rarely, from previously observed extremes.

Over long periods of time, however, in any given geographical location, weather occasionally exceeds the limits dictated by climatic records. A dozen or more temperature and precipitation records may unexpectedly fall during a week of exceptional weather.

The infinite variety and novelty continuously exhibited by the weather -- not to mention its potential for disaster -- keeps people involved. People like to follow the daily weather. Some like to keep track of it, measure it, catagorize it and record it. Most like to talk, and read and write about it.

Weather records of sorts go back several centuries, but continuous, reliable records, upon which we base our climatic statistics, exist for only the last 100 years -- many for less than 50 years. We have not, during this very small segment of geological time, experienced all the weather extremes possible for the climatic period in which we live. Therefore, small departures from normal or expected conditions do not necessarily herald an overall change in local or regional climate. More likely they indicate an inadequate period of record in which to observe the extremes possible within our current climatic regime.

While ordinary people forget the weather that occurred last week, climatologists don't because they keep statistics. They maintain daily, weekly, monthly, seasonal, annual, decadal and 30 year normals (averages) plus a battery of more arcane statistical tools. They find these devices useful, even necessary, for describing past weather. Unfortunately, to the average person who can sense hot or cold but not a normal temperature, they have little meaning.

Statistics generally mask the innumerable details that make up the real weather and therefore offer little appreciation, or even comprehension, for the milieu or ambiance of a locality or an event. Only an anecdotal first hand report of a visitor, hopefully a poet, can possibly recapture, recreate and transmit a sense of participation; of actually reliving and savoring the exhilaration prompted by a spring day; or experiencing the bite of windchill;

or suffering the lethargy of a muggy summer afternoon. Statistics cannot replace the perceptions and emotions that derive from personal involvement.

For example, cloudy days, often warmer than average in the morning and colder than average in the afternoon, invoke feelings of coldness -- although the day's temperature may average exactly normal. Conversely, a clear, dry day with chilly morning temperatures will warm considerable during the day and may conjure up a feeling of warmth even when the day averages below normal.

A person may perceive a day with exactly average morning and afternoon temperatures as either cold or warm depending on recent conditions (acclimation). In spring, after a long cold spell, any temperature increase induces a sense of warmth and well being.

Thus, a large gap exists between dynamic, exciting and outright freakish "real' weather and dry statistical accounts of past temperature and rainfall averages and extremes. Never-the-less, statistical (as opposed to descriptive) climate has its uses. No one can begin to remember all the weather experienced in a lifetime. It would require a large library to maintain a descriptive log for just the noteworthy events. Practically speaking, without using numbers, we cannot possibly describe the myriad manifestations and guises our weather assumes. To make this task manageable, we reduce the weather to a numerical description and express it statistically in terms of averages, means and extremes.

Because we maintain such an avid interest in weather, past, present and future, we make the effort to record and preserve daily and hourly weather data for thousands of cities and towns around the world. Although we lose much in the process, it permits us to easily compare certain features of current and past weather -- and to watch for changing climate.

CLIMATE AND LORE

We find the earliest concept of climate in the lore of primeval civilizations that depended mainly on agriculture, and therefore the weather, for their livelihood. Over the millennia, they anxiously watched the skies and waited for the life-supporting winter and spring rains, followed by the dry warmth of summer and autumn. In time, they noticed that certain conditions seemed to presage better or worse than ideal weather for their crops. Their attempts to define the normal, expected, weather for their locality -- and to predict situations where it would significantly deviate from the average -- evolved into an accumulation of weather wisdom that we now call weather lore, weather proverbs and weather sayin's.

During the renaissance, meteorological instruments (thermometers, barometers and many varieties of the anemometer) became available and found their way into Northern Europe -- particularly into the larger cities with universities. In time, instruments improved and became more generally available but, until the late 18th century, thermometers and barometers remained mainly in the hands of professors, ministers and amateur investigators of the wealthy or educated classes.

The instruments that existed had no uniformity in design, manufacture or even scale. Individuals could but read their instruments, apply the time-honored proverbs and folklore handed down by word of mouth or printed in the almanacs of the day, and make their own weather forecast.

Little coordination or exchange of data occurred between investigators and climatology remained a descriptive process. Travelers such as Marco Polo would return from their journeys with subjective descriptions of the weather in other lands couched in terms of their own climate e.g. colder, wetter.

Between 1337 and 1344, an unknown Englishman maintained a daily record of weather and wind direction. This earliest known (in the western hemisphere) meteorological record survives, remarkably, while most others have perished. Remaining records for the time before the 16th century exist as fragmentary, anecdotal, accounts of floods, droughts, heat waves and cold spells. In some instances, historians have melded such anecdotal accounts of weather with sporadic fragments of temperature data to synthesize a climatic record reaching back to the 17th century. The record, however, remains anything but complete.

In 1660, the Royal Society recognized the need to keep a "history of the weather" and commissioned Robert Hook to devise a plan for recording daily weather observations. Accordingly, while most mainland European weather records from the 17th century have perished, an unbroken sequence of daily observations for the London area reaches back to 1668. Meteorological records for Berlin go back to 1719. In Italy, observations from the "Tuscan network" began in 1654 when Ferdinand II distributed thermometers to a number of locations in Tuscany. The network operated for 13 years but, unfortunately, most of the records disappeared. The Italians took no further synoptic observations until 1855.

The thermometer apparently reached China around 1670 but Chinese climatology began many centuries before instrumentation. A description of the "monsoon climate" appeared in Chinese literature during the Han dynasty of the 2nd and 3rd centuries A.D. The Chinese based their early climatology on phenological observations that related distinctive climatic periods (seasons) to important phases of plant growth.

Chinese observers began to keep modern weather records in Shanghai in 1873 and in Hon Kong in 1884. The interruption of World War II temporarily broke the continuous documentation between 1939 and 1946. After the war the quality and quantity of weather observations slowly improved.

In the New World, luminaries such as Benjamin Franklin and Thomas Jefferson maintained careful climatic records. However, at the outbreak of the American Revolutionary War, fewer than 100 thermometers existed in all of Colonial America. Of the individual records kept, many perished in cataclysmic disasters such as fire, flood and war.

Even well into the 19th century, government authorities made little or no effort to initiate routine weather observations. Finally, in mid-19th century, groups of scientific investigators began a general effort to gather and maintain weather records. In the 1870s and 1880s, American and European atmospheric researchers developed extensive data-gathering networks on their own initiative. Although they compiled data mainly to study storm development, their accumulated records became the seed of modern climatology.

CLASSIFYING CLIMATES

The ancient Greeks devised the earliest system of climate classification. Based on the simple relationship between latitude and temperature, they divided the earth into broad east-west zones (called klima). This scheme ultimately led to a three-tier classification based on three basic latitudinal zones -- The hot, humid equatorial region bounded by the Tropics of Cancer and Capricorn; the cold polar regions north and south of the Arctic and Antarctic Circles; and the relatively moderate zones in between. Originally called the "summerless," "intermediate" and "winterless," we now know them as the "Frigid," "Temperate" and "Torrid" Zones. Although it ignores factors other than latitude, this simple form of climate classification persisted well into modern times.

Modern climatology teaches us that the cumulative effect of elevation, topography, moisture availability and latitude maintain the different climates (characteristic weather) we experience when traveling around the world. Most climatologists, however, now express the various climate classes in terms of temperature and precipitation -- the two elements most important to vegetation and human comfort.

In 1884, Alexander Supan, a German climatologist, produced the first major improvement to the mathematical, zonal, climate scheme. Using observed rather than theoretical temperatures, he developed a global climatology that defined 34 different climatic provinces. He based his groupings mainly on temperature and rainfall but partly on wind and the local terrain.

In 1900, Wladimir Köppen, a Russian-German climatologist, introduced a novel method that used patterns of vegetation and soils to classify climate. Since the dominant natural vegetation of any region survives only within certain limits of sunlight, temperature, precipitation, humidity, soil moisture, and wind, Köppen reasoned that the native plant life of a region could uniquely define its climatology.

Köppen used precise temperature and precipitation averages to define the boundaries of climatic regions containing similar vegetation and soils. He labled the five major climate groups with capital letters; (A) for tropical rainy climates, (B) for dry climates, (C) for humid moderate-temperature (mesothermal) climates, (D) for humid low-temperature (microthermal) climates and (E) for polar, snow climates. He subdivided each major climate zone, using lower case letters to delineate seasonal variations and regions tending toward extremes in precipitation and/or temperature.

Most modern climatologies classify climatic regions according to the effects local temperature and precipitation have on plant and animal life -- and sometimes on terrain. Plants in a hot-humid region need more precipitation than those in a cool-humid region because the warmer region has a higher evaporation rate. A ten-inch average annual rainfall might well support a coniferous forest in a cool climate but only desert shrubs in a warm one. Temperature and precipitation act in concert to produce a climate type.

A refinement of Wladimir Köppen's basic system, introduced by the United States climatologist C. Warren Thornthwaite in 1931, defined five climate types found around the world that feature comparably humidity and vegetation; wet rain forest, humid forest, subhumid grassland, semiarid steppe, and arid desert. He sub-divided each type into vegetation-temperature categories; tropical, mesothermal, microthermal, taiga, tundra, and frost.

The geographic-vegetative approach to climate developed by Köppen and modified by Thornthwaite provide a detailed, understandable and practical classification of global climatic. Such a climatology quickly reveals that a traveler from Savannah, Georgia, would feel quite at home, climatically if not culturally, in Shanghai, China.

CHANGING CLIMATE

The advent of a safe, workable steam engine in 1712, produced the great Industrial Revolution of the 18th and 19th centuries. Steam ran the machines, but coal fueled the steam engines. Industrial furnaces, consuming great quantities of coal, belched forth huge clouds of dense black smoke into the atmosphere. Before long, near-suffocating combinations of smoke and fog -- "smogs" -- hung like a pall over industrial areas such as England and the northeastern United States. In 1952, a smothering blanket of smog contributed to the death of more than 4000 persons in London.

Aside from the large and very obvious particles of soot, the burning coal lofted sulfur, carbon dioxide and other noxious chemicals and gases into the air. In the late 1800s, the visionary Swedish Chemist, Svante Arrhenius, seeing beyond the deadly smoke, cautioned the world that accumulations of carbon dioxide in the atmosphere would warm the earth by some nine degrees (F) by the end of the 20th century, with possible dire consequences. Everyone, of course, ignored Arrhenius -- until lately.

A long cooling trend that began in the 1940s and continued into the 1970s convinced many climatologists that indeed the earth would decline into a new Ice Age within a few thousand years. Then, in the 1970s, the earth's temperature began to rise. After a string of record breaking hot years in the late 1980s and early 1990s, scientists began to re-evaluate their position on global climate.

Apparently human industries have dramatically increased the concentrations of carbon dioxide, methane and other gases such as nitrous oxide and chloroflorocarbons in the atmosphere since the end of World War

II. As predicted by Arrhenius, these gases have apparently trapped an increasingly large amount of the earth's surface heat. The increase in heat has consequently increased the amount of water vapor (another greenhouse heat-trap) in the atmosphere. Most climatologists now agree that these events have produced a global warming trend that, if continued, carries potentially grim environmental problems.

The gigantic explosion of Mt. Pinatubo in the Philippines in June, 1991, temporarily interrupted the warming. The eruption lofted millions of tons of dust, smoke, sulfur gases and other contaminants into the stratosphere. The global warming of the 1980s and early 1990s quickly reversed as the shroud of pollutants encircled the earth and reflected sunlight back into space. After about two years, however, the aerosols from Mt. Pinatubo settled out and global temperatures once again edged upward.

THE CLIMATE-WARMING DEBATE

According to atmospheric theory, large increases of carbon dioxide and other "greenhouse" gases in the air must continue to increase the surface temperature of the earth.

Climate computer models indicate that greenhouse warming should have warmed the earth at least three degrees Fahrenheit in the last century. However, the best analysis of observed temperatures over the last 100 years indicated only a one degree increase at most. Unable to determine the reason for the discrepancy in predicted and actual temperature rise, researchers could not state categorically that human activities had induced the warming trend -- or if the trend would continue. Serious debate over the global warming issue raged throughout the scientific community, leading to confusion and skepticism among the general populace.

As they later discovered, pollutants (called aerosols) thrown into the air by burning fossil fuels, reflect enough sunlight back into space to nearly counteract the warming caused by the increase in greenhouse gases. When researchers factored in the "aerosol effect," the computer models predicted that the earth should have warmed about one degree Fahrenheit -- close to the observed warming.

The new computer results prompted a UN sponsored International Panel of Climate Change (IPCC), comprising over 1,500 leading climate experts, to issue a consensus opinion that the earth's climate has indeed warmed and, under current conditions, would continue to warm at an even greater rate in the future. The U.S. National Academy of Sciences concurred, estimating a further two to six degree Fahrenheit leap in global temperature if atmospheric concentrations of carbon dioxide should double in the next 50 years.

Thomas Karl of the National Climatic Data Center in Ashville, North Carolina, who wrote part of the IPCC report, placed the probability that a significant warming has occurred in the range of 90 to 95 percent. In addition, he and other researchers have detected anomalies in weather occurrences -- above-normal winter precipitation, severe droughts in summer, heavier rainstorms and reduced day-to-day temperature variations -- since the mid-1970's. These anomalies bear the "signature of greenhouse warming." It seems that we can expect strange weather to occur along with greenhouse warming.

The apocalypse of global warming, especially as characterized in the popular media, contains such doomsday scenarios as continuous heat waves with 95 degree temperatures that begin in June and continue through September. Under attack from this withering heat, forests die, ecosystems vanish and food supplies dwindle. Severe drought and monster tropical storms like Hugo and Andrew occur more frequently and, as glaciers melt, rising seas claim huge swaths of densely populated coast land.

While expressing consensus about the reality of global warming, many experts still confess uncertainty regarding the earth's ultimate reaction to a warming trend. Climate responds to a number of environmental parameters that either force climate change or react, in concert with or opposition to, a climate change. Eventually scientists will discover all the parameters involved and determine which initiate, which oppose and which abet climatic warming. Then we may begin to develop countermeasures against further warming -- or learn how to live with it.

THE PENDING ICE AGE

Although global warming has our immediate attention, a few decades ago the main concern of climatologists involved the onset of the next ice age. Archeological studies of previous ice ages indicate that interglacial periods have relatively short live spans -- about 20,000 years. Climatologists think our present interglacial, the Holocene, has passed the midpoint of its life span and we can expect the earth to begin its slide into the clutches of another full-blown ice age within the next 2000 years.

The Milankovitch astronomical theory of Ice Ages indicates that changes in the earth's orbit about the sun and the tilt of the earth's axis of rotation are currently at work to cool the climate -- with or without anthropomorphically induced greenhouse warming.

CHAPTER THIRTEEN

A HISTORY OF ICE AGES

Wherein we examine the large changes in climate that have, over the eons, produced the long periods of glaciation -- the Ice Ages -- that have plagued the earth and its various life forms for the past 65 million years, and especially the last two million years. We also examine the techniques by which climate detectives have determined how and when the great glaciers visited the earth and explore some of the possible causes of these catastrophic events.

"We now know that the recent Ice Age has consisted of many intervals of glacial expansion that have been separated by warmer interglacial intervals, including the one in which we almost certainly live today. There is no reason to believe that the Ice Age has ended."
    -- Steven M. Stanley

ICE AGES

Europe, once lush with tropical vegetation where oversized elephants browsed, became suddenly inundated by a thick sheet of ice. The rapid advance of the ice sheets encroaching from the north drove away or obliterated all life forms save perhaps some bacteria, algae and other primitive forms of life. At its greatest extent, the monstrous one-mile thick blanket of ice covered Scandinavia, most of Great Britain, Denmark, northern Germany and Russia as far south as Moscow. Ice spread also from the Alps to cover the Swiss plain, the Jura mountain range and parts of France, Germany and Austria.

In the Americas, a similar mantle of glacial ice pushed out from Canada into the eastern and Midwestern states. From the Rocky mountain and Cascade ranges, ice spread into northern Washington, Idaho and Montana. In the southern hemisphere, small glaciers covered the southern Andes mountains and parts of Australia and New Zealand as well.

THE LEGACY OF THE ICE

After about 100,000 years, as mysteriously as it began, the ice began to melt. By 10,000 years ago, only small vestiges of the great ice sheets remained near the north and south poles. However, the fantastically destructive glaciers left monuments of evidence, attesting to their existence, that even 10,000 years of weathering could not entirely obliterate.

As glaciers grow and move they scrape up and carry with them enormous quantities of sand, gravel and even large boulders. A moving glacier, with its load of rock fragments, acts like a giant rasp or file, grinding away the bedrock, leaving long scratches or grooves in the polished surface. During glacial retreat the ice melts, leaving their accumulated debris (called till) behind them. These deposits of sand, gravel and rock indicate not only the past occurrance of a glacier but also the extreme limit of encroachment.

Glaciers can carry huge blocks of granite that no other erosional agent could possibly budge. When a glacier retreats, it leaves these giant boulders (called erratics) lying about in regions far from any possible local source.

THE EVIDENCE

The beginning of modern glaciology began, perhaps not surprisingly, in Switzerland where people live and work in close proximity to glaciers. Swiss farmers could not help but notice the erratic boulders sitting in highly unlikely places. They also puzzled over the parallel hills of gravel and rock and the long lakes that covered the outwash plains. People living near mountains wondered what caused the scratches and grooves that marred the otherwise highy polished granite bedrock.

Having no memory of the great Ice Age -- nor the experience or imagination to conjure up anything like the true reason for such curiosities -- most geologists assumed that the great biblical deluge had deposited the erratics and sediments and fashioned the oddly arranged landscape. But not all.

As early as 1787, a Swiss minister, Bernard Friedrich Kuhn, correctly assumed that past episodes of moving glaciers had deposited the erratic boulders. A few years later a Scottish geologist, James Hutton, reached the same conclusion as Kuhn after visiting the Swiss Jura mountain region.

THE FATHER OF MODERN GEOLOGY

Geologists now regard James Hutton as the founder of modern geological science. Although he obtained a medical degree in 1749, he never practiced medicine. Instead, he became interested in agricultural chemistry and later in minerology and geology. He made a fortune manufacturing ammonium chloride and retired in 1768 to devote himself exclusively to geology.

In his walks over the English countryside he observed that different forms of rocks -- some laid down as sediment and compressed and hardened and others brought to the surface in liquid form (lava) and hardened as they cooled -- all showed signs of slow weathering from wind and water.

In Hutton's day most perople, even scientists, believed the earth had been created a mere 6,000 years earlier. Hutton, however, realized that it would require a much longer time for wind and rain to errode and weather the rocks into their current shapes. It therefore appeared obvious that, contrary to conventional beliefs of the time, the earth had existed for much longer than 6,000 years and had slowly evolved into its present form.

In 1785 Hutton published his views in a book, *Theory of Earth*. Since the book contained the general principles of modern geology, science now regards him as the "father of geology."

Hutton's interest in nature also extended to meteorology. In his book he noted that the amount of moisture (water vapor) that air can hold depends on its temperature. Consequently, he observed, when a warm air mass encounters a cold one, its temperature decreases and it can no longer hold as much moisture as before. Some of the moisture therefore precipitates out as rain. In this light perhaps we should also consider James Hutton as the "father of modern meteorology."

GLACIAL THEORY

In the early 1800s, Reinhard Bernhardi, a German professor of natural science, after observing evidence of former glaciers in Norway, advanced the theory that the polar ice-cap had once spread outward as far south as central Germany.

Most scientists of the day, however, clung to the conventional theory that, during the great biblical flood of Noah's time, currents of water carrying mud and rocks had made the marks and grooves in the mountains, and boulder-laden icebergs, drifted around on the flood waters, had dropped the erractics. In 1833, the imminent English geologist, Charles Lyell, formally introduced the "ice-raft" theory in opposition to Bernhardi's embryonic "glacial theory."

Around 1815, a Swiss mountaineer, Jean-Pierre Perraudin, more curious than most, inspected a group of marks and grooves close to the Val de Bagnes glacier in the southern Swiss Alps. He concluded that the glacier had once filled the entire valley and had made the marks as it slowly pushed its load of rock and gravel forward through the valley.

Perraudin pressed his conclusion on to all who would listen. Eventually he convinced a highway and bridge engineer, Ignace Venetz, that, indeed, moving glaciers had made the marks in the granite bedrock and had carried the huge erratic boulders into far-flung fields. Venetz formally presented the theory to the Swiss Society of Natural Sciences at Bern in 1829.

Although he failed to convince many of the attendees, Venetz did convince the naturalist, Jean de Charpentier. Interestingly enough, Charpentier had once also talked to Perraudin but had considered the hypothesis less than probable. On this second exposure, he became convinced and placed his considerable support behind Venetz.

Charpentier then converted another doubter, Louis Agassiz, to the glacial theory. As one of Europe's foremost men of science, and a charismatic and forceful speaker in the bargain, Agassiz quickly became a major emissary in the advancement of glacial theory. His convincing book, *Studies on Glaciers*, published in 1840, focused the attention of the scientific world on the issue of ancient glaciation.

ICE AGES -- YES, BUT WHY?

As the theory of ancient widespread glaciation gained converts, scientists began mounting global expeditions to find additional clues to their existence -- and to learn more about how glaciers form and how they work. Even with the rudimentary dating techniques available at the time, it soon became obvious that glaciers have visited the earth not once but on several occasions. In a next logical step, they began to search for causes of the seemingly random episodes of large-scale glaciation.

It seemed reasonable to assume that massive glacial growth would require a substantial decrease in global temperature. Over the years geologists and climatologists have advanced several theories -- some testable and others not testable or not easily testable -- that might cause the necessary drop in temperature.

A decrease in radiation from the sun, by whatever means, could cause the earth to cool significantly. However, the most sophisticated instruments yet available have not conclusively uncovered any systematic fluctuations in the sun's luminosity.

Scientists have considered other, more mechanical situations that could reduce the sun's output -- possibly some mechanism that attenuates solar radiation enroute to the earth, or some change in the earth's atmosphere that would absorb or reflect the radiation.

The list of usual suspects always includes volcanic erruptions which throw great concentrations of chemicals and dust into the atmosphere. The pollutants absorb radiation and reflect sunlight back into space. Cooling attributed to the gigantic 1991 Pinatubo eruption in the Philippines completely reversed the record warming trend of the early 1990s for two years.

As the Solar System travels through its tiny part of the galaxy, it encounters varying amounts of cosmic gas and dust. Should we enter a very dusty region, the earth could experience a sharp decrease in solar radiation.

None of these explanations, either individually or in combination, provided a complete explanation of why glaciers begin and end. They especially do not explain why they occur in periodic episodes.

ASTRONOMICAL INFLUENCES ON CLIMATE

Since Babylonian times, astronomers have known that the earth's axis of rotation tilts about 24 degrees from a vertical line through the orbital plane. The Greek astronomer, Hipparchus, discovered that the axis of rotation gradually swings in a circle over a period of about 22,000 years. In the 17th century, the astronomer, Johann Kepler, determined that the earth, and all the planets, followed an elliptical orbit about the sun. He also observed that the sun occupied one of the two focal points. In 1843, the great French astronomer, Urbain Leverrier, determined that the earth's orbit changed from a nearly circular configuration to a slightly elongated one every 100,000 years. As the orbit elongates, the focal points move farther apart, causing the earth's distance from the sun to vary during each passage around the sun. Thus, by the 19th century, researchers had already discovered all the components necessary to construct an "astronomical theory" of climate change. It required only some visionary to assemble the parts into a coherent hypothesis.

In 1842, a French mathematician, Joseph Alphonse Adhémar, first suggested that variations in the tilt of the earth's axis as it orbits the sun could modify the amount of sunshine reaching the earth and affect the global climate.

In 1864, James Croll, a self-taught scientist with an obsession for understanding nature, studied Leverrier's orbital calculations and hypothesized that variations in the shape of the earth's orbit might cause significant changes in global temperature and cause glaciers to wax and wane.

He surmised that, during periods when the orbit reached greater eccentricity (elongation) the earth would move farther from the sun. The cooler temperatures would cause additional snow to fall. Any small increase in the area covered by snow would cause additional cooling by reflecting heat back into space. The change in the snowpack would therefore amplify the effect of an astronomically induced decrease in solar radiation. Croll thus introduced the first example of "positive feedback" into the science of climatology.

Croll's reasoned theory caught the attention of Sir Archibald Geikie, the Director of the Geological Survey in Scotland, who offered Croll a position. Croll accepted and continued his research on the astronomical theory of ice ages. In 1875 he published an advanced theory that also considered

Adhémar's tilt of the earth's axis of rotation, as well as the changes in eccentricity of the earth's orbit around the sun, as probable causes of ice ages. The discovery of multiple past glacial episodes argued in favor of a cyclical, and therefore an astronomical cause. However 19th century techniques for dating glacial episodes could not adequately prove or disprove Croll's theories. When meteorologists stated that Croll's variations in solar heating could not provide the necessary heating or cooling to cause a major global climate change, geologists generally abandoned the astronomical theory.

A generation later, a Serbian astronomer, Milutin Milankovitch, revived Croll's theory.

THE ASTRONOMICAL THEORY OF ICE AGES

During the 1920s and 1930s, Milankovitch worked to develop a mathematical theory that would explain all present and past climates of the earth -- and of Mars and Venus as well.

In his research, he discovered the hypotheses of Adhémar and Croll. Both had advanced theories that variations in the earth's tilt and orbit could affect the earth's climate. Neither, however, had the mathematical skill to accurately calculate the magnitude of change possible.

Milankovitch investigated the tilt of the earth's axis of rotation and the precession of the tilt but, for some reason, failed to include orbital considerations. In 1920 he published his landmark contribution to modern climatology, the *Mathematical Theory of Heat Phenomena Produced by Solar Radiation*. His book demonstrated that small cyclical variations in the earth's spin as it orbits the sun, could cause significant changes in the distribution and intensity of sunlight falling upon the earth. This could lead to dramatic fluctuations in the global climate -- especially the Northern Hemisphere.

According to the Milankovitch theory, individual changes -- and combinations of changes -- in the degree of tilt of the earth's axis of rotation, and the revolution of the axial tilt, combine to cause slow but distinct oscillations of the earth's climate with periods of about 41,000 years (from the degree of tilt), and about 23,000 years (from revolution of the tilt).

THE TILT

Consider a flat plane passing through both the center of the earth and the center of the sun. Although the plane teeters slightly up and down, the earth, in its yearly orbit around the sun remains on this plane -- appropriately called the orbital plane.

As we know that the earth *revolves* about the sun and, at the same time, spins *(rotates)* once each day upon its axis. By some marvel of design or happenstance, the earth's axis of rotation tilts (currently 23-½ degrees) with respect to a vertical line through the orbital plane.

This propitious tilt causes the seasons. While sunlight bathes fully half the earth's surface at any given moment, some regions near the north and south poles receive little or no sunlight for portions of the year owing to the tilt of rotation. With the current tilt, the equatorial regions receive a full 12 hours of sunlight each day while the polar regions receive a varying amount -- ranging from near zero to near 24 hours, according to the season. During the course of a human lifetime, the tilt remains essentially constant with respect to the orbital plane.

As the earth journeys around the sun, it continuously presents a different facet of its geography to the sun. At one end of the orbit, when the northern hemisphere tilts toward the sun, the increase in solar radiation in the northern latitudes brings summer (summer solstice). At the other end, when it tilts away from the sun, little light reaches the northern latitudes. Then we have winter (Winter solstice) and the southern hemisphere has summer. At the half-way points (approximately) between winter and summer we have autumn (autumnal equinox) and spring (spring equinox).

Over a period of 41,000 years, the tilt of the axis actually varies from a minimum of 22 degrees to a maximum of 25 degrees. Seasonal changes become more intense during periods of maximum tilt. In about 20,000 years the tilt will reach its minimum which should reflect in a slight moderation of seasonal extremes.

Owing to the gravitational pull of the sun and the moon, the earth's axis of rotation slowly revolves (called the precession of Earth's axial tilt). In the course of time the axis of rotation will describe a complete circle on the celestial sphere. During the course of its precession, the axis, which now points toward Polaris, will point progressively to other stars and eventually point once again toward the Pole Star.

The precession of the axial tilt causes another precession -- the precession of the seasons. Northern hemisphere winter begins on or about December 21st when the axis of rotation tilts exactly away from the sun. Northern hemisphere summer begins on or about June 21st when the earth reaches the other end of the orbit and the axis of rotation tilts exactly toward the sun.

In about 11,000 years, however, the earth's axis of rotation will have precessed such that it tilts away from the sun on June 21st and the northern hemisphere will have winter when they once had summer. This fact, while interesting, would have little impact on the overall climate if not for the physical geography of the earth.

EARTH'S INFLUENCE ON CLIMATE CHANGE

It appears likely that the cause of glacial episodes on earth lies partially with the physical geography of the northern and southern hemispheres and partially with variations of the earth's axis of rotation.

The tropical regions receive the largest share of solar radiation and the polar regions the least. Although atmospheric and oceanic circulations partially correct this imbalance of energy, the tropics still receive more energy than they lose each year while the polar regions lose more than they gain.

Land masses radiate heat back to space much faster than ocean surfaces. Since by far most of the earth's land lies in the northern hemisphere, the earth radiates more heat into space during northern hemisphere winters than during southern hemisphere winters. Moreover, winter snow accumulates on land surfaces but not on ocean surfaces excepting the Arctic Sea which freezes solid in winter. Accumulated snow and ice reflect a substantial amount of incoming solar radiation. The greater loss of heat from radiation and reflection intensifies northern hemisphere winters.

If the earth had no irregular features such as continents and mountains, atmospheric pressure, temperature, precipitation and winds would presumably become arranged in zonal belts that parallel the equator. In fact, atmospheric circulation in the southern hemisphere, which lacks serious obstacles to horizontal air flow, does approach such a zonal arrangement.

The northern hemisphere, however, contains huge land masses with large mountain ranges. These features breakdown the zonal belts of pressure and wind which, in turn, greatly complicate atmospheric and oceanic circulation patterns and thus temperature and precipitation patterns.

Despite these complications, the global circulation usually remains sufficiently regular and dependable to produce a global pattern of recognizable and classifiable climatic features. Unless, of course, an outside influence such as a change in the radiation received by the earth's surface upsets the balance of forces that control the climate.

No fewer than five different earth systems combine to influence climate; the atmosphere, the biosphere, the hydrosphere, the cryosphere and the pedosphere. Each operates on a different time-scale and the impact of each varies substantially. Moreover, each may produce corresponding changes in one or more of the other four. Gradual changes between of one or more of the five operators may produce significant changes in local climate, or even global climate over a period of time.

The atmosphere responds most quickly to external forces such as daily or seasonal variations in solar radiation. It responds slowly to man-made or natural emissions at the surface and more slowly to stratospheric pollution caused by volcanic eruptions, aircraft emissions and solar eruptions.

Changes in the biosphere usually reflect changes in atmospheric circulation. Since the advent of civilization, however, humankind (an increasingly significant force within the biosphere) has wrought significant changes in the biosphere through agriculture, deforestation and urbanization. Such changes can, and likely will, affect atmospheric circulation patterns through large changes in the earth's global temperature.

The hydrosphere includes all the liquid water on earth. The oceans, however, play the crucial role in regulating (and changing) the climate. Oceans absorb the bulk of the solar radiation that falls on the earth. The suns energy vaporizes water from the surface which ascends into the atmosphere, condenses into clouds that drift into the extratropical regions. Ultimately, the water vapor and its associated latent heat, precipitates out as life-sustaining rain and warmth. Ocean currents also transport heat from tropical to polar regions.

The cryosphere includes all portions of the earth's surface whose average temperature remains consistently below the freezing point of water. Such conditions, usually found in the polar regions, also exist at higher elevations in the temperate and tropical regions. Snow and ice in these regions reflect much of the solar radiation they receive and substantially reduce the surface heating.

Small changes in the cryospheric occur seasonally, but major variations occur over centuries or millennia.

The pedosphere, the solid portion of the earth's surface that lies above sea level, has evolved over millions of years through the process of continental drift or plate tectonics. Continents, especially the ice covered portions, reflect more solar radiation than oceans. Thus the earth grows colder when continents drift into polar regions and warmer when they drift into equatorial regions.

NEW EVIDENCE

In time, the majority of geologists came to favor Milankovitch's theory, contradicting evidence not withstanding. Primary objections centered around an inability to fit some observed geological data to the Milankovitch theory. Some said the discrepancies disproved the theory while others questioned the geological chronology determined by questionable dating techniques.

In the late 1940s, Willard F. Libby developed a new technique for dating the remains of organic material. Cosmic rays entering the atmosphere produce small quantities of radioactive carbon (called radiocarbon) within the atmosphere. All living organisms absorb a certain amount of radiocarbon while they live. After death, the radiocarbon begins to disintegrate at a known rate into inert atoms of nitrogen. The ratio of radiocarbon to nitrogen in a fossil therefore provides the length of time since the organism died -- and therefore the approximate date it lived.

The discovery, by the new radioactive carbon technology, of a 25,000 year-old peat bog in Illinois shattered the Milankovitch theory. According to Milankovitch calculations, a cold period, during which peat bogs could not form in Illionis, should have occurred 25,000 years ago. By the mid-1950s, geologists and glaciologists (and meteorologists) had generally discarded the astronomical theory as a viable cause of Ice Ages.

By 1970, owing to much improved geological dating techniques, the situation had once again reversed and the majority of geologists and glaciologists re-embraced the basic tenets of the Milankovitch astronomical theory.

EVIDENCE FROM THE SEA AND THE ICE

Even in the 19th century, scientists knew more about the surface of the moon than they did about the bottom of the sea. In the late 1800s, the British government equipped a ship to take ocean depth soundings, collect samples of ocean water, plants and animals, and dredge the ocean bottom. For three years the expedition probed the depths of the world's oceans and returned with vast quantities of data and information.

An international team of investigators analyzed the data and, in 1895, published a 50-volume report. Of the staggering volume of data, paleoclimatologists found of particular interest the evidence that some species of ocean plants and animals (known collectively as plankton) lived only in cold water while other species lived only in warm water. Thus, it appeared, the layers of undisturbed sea-floor sediment could provide a climatic history for the earth reaching back hundreds of thousands of years.

SEA-SEDIMENT CORES

Then as now, drifting along in the upper layers of the ocean, an incredibly diverse group of microscopic plants and animals live, reproduce and die by the billions each day. As they die, their remains drift down through the murky depths and accumulate on the ocean floor. Growing by an inch or so every thousand years, this steady rain of debris has produced a blanket of sediment hundreds of yards deep.

A thin layer of deep-sea sediment contains the remains of thousands of plankton animals (called foraminifera or forams) and billions of coccoliths (minute calcite scales of algal cells that live upon the surfaces of the foraminiferas). Long sediment cores, of the order of ten yards, contain forams that lived over 100 million years ago. The chemistry of the fossil skeletons at various layers through the core reveal the state of the seawater, and therefore information about the environment that existed, when and where the organisms lived.

For example, sea water contains two distinct types (isotopes) of oxygen atoms; a heavy type that contains two extra neutrons (oxygen-18) and a lighter type (oxygen-16). During the process of evaporation, molecules containing the lighter oxygen-16 escape more easily from the sea surface than those containing the heavier oxygen-18.

During glacial periods, a substantial amount of precipitation falls as snow and accumulates on the glaciers. This removes some water, along with its complement of Oxygen-16, from the ocean and stores it in glacial ice. Thus, ice-age oceans contain a higher concentration of the Oxygen-18 isotope. The depletion of pure water through glaciation leaves the oceans with a higher degree of salinity. During warm, interglacial periods the glaciers melt, the Oxygen-16 isotope and the fresh water return to the oceans restoring the origional composition.

Organisms living in cold water incorporate a higher ratio of the heavier isotope, Oxygen-18, into their skeleton during their life. The ratio of oxygen-18 to oxygen-16 in a fossil skeleton therefore reveals the sea water temperature that existed when the animal or plant lived. Scientists measuring the ratio of oxygen-18 to oxygen-16 in the fossil skeletons at successive depths in the sea-sediment can thereby calculate the water temperature that existed during the lifetime of the organism, and reconstruct the climatic evolution over past eons.

The reaction of one species of plankton to changing environmental conditions provides a simple illustration of the complex interactions that may occur between the biosphere, the hydrosphere and the atmosphere during major changes in climate.

Researchers find the plankton animal, *Globorotalia menardii*, exclusively in sea-sediment cores taken from lower, and therefore warmer, latitudes. As climate changes, the geographic extend of these temperature-sensitive organisms shift accordingly. It therefore appeared that fluctuations in *menardii* abundance in various sedimentary layers at any given location provided a clear record of ancient sea-water temperature changes.

However, as it turned out, *menardii's* sensitivity to increases in the ocean's salinity, rather than ocean temperature, caused it to appear and disappear.

Cooler Ice-Age temperatures cause an increase in the oceans salinity by locking up a sizeable portion of pure water in glaciers. Since glacial growth causes an increase in salinity, which causes *menardii* to decrease or disappear, the quantity of *menardii* contained in various layers of sea-floor sediment must therefore directly reflect the amount of *glacial ice* on the earth at the time rather than the temperature.

GLACIAL ICE CORES

As with sea-sediments, the ratio of oxygen isotopes in ice cores extracted from glaciers can reveal the progression of climate changes. Recently, researchers have examined cores extracted from depths two miles below the surface of the great ice caps of Greenland and Antarctica.

By examining the temperature of the cores and analyzing the dust, air bubbles, acidity and oxygen isotopes contained within the cores, researchers can piece together a fairly detailed and accurate climate history. The Greenland and Antarctica ice cores yield data that dates back 250,000 and 500,000 years respectively.

Evidence from the ice confirms that from the sediments. A graph of isotopic measurements made on two Indian Ocean cores reflect variations in the volume of global ice over the last 500 thousand years. The record reveals major climate changes every 100,000 years with other, minor, fluctuations every 41,000 years and 22,000 years.

Records from ice cores taken at various places around the world indicate that an Ice Age cycle begins with a sudden surge of glacial growth followed by a slow recovery that takes about 100,000 years. The long recovery period contains two additional sharp but shorter lived glacial increases that also occur cyclically -- one at 43,000 years, and a second that modulates between 19,000 and 23,000 years.

In addition, other smaller fluctuations of glacial growth and decay occur -- caused, we now assume, by various combinations of astronomical influence and modified by interactions of physical processes occurring between the earth's atmosphere, hydrosphere, biosphere, cryosphere and pedosphere.

The glacial cycle culminates in a relatively short interglacial period of warmth such as we now have.

ANOTHER ASTRONOMICAL PARAMETER

Milankovitch had not uncovered the 100,000 year cycle of Pleistocene ice ages. Almost immediately, however, scientists attributed it to the 100,000 year changes in orbital eccentricity first advanced by Croll.

In 1973, James Hays confirmed the existence of the 100,000 year climate cycle. He analyzed a sea-sediment core that contained a detailed record of climate extending back for 450,000 years. When he compared the climate cycles to recently recalculated astronomical curves, the 100,000 year cycle stood out as the dominant cycle with the 41,000 year and the 23,000 year cycles superimposed upon it.

ORBITAL ECCENTRICITY

The earth's orbit about the sun describes a rather fat ellipse which segues from slightly elongated (eccentric) to nearly circular over a period of about 100,000 years. The earth experiences the greatest variations in solar radiation, and thus in climate, at times of greatest eccentricity and the least variation at times of least eccentricity (nearly circular orbit).

An ellipse has two axes, one long and one short, and two focal points (foci) that grow farther apart as the ellipse gains eccentricity. The sun lies at one of the focal points rather than at the geometric center of the ellipse. Thus, the earth moves successively closer to (perihelion) and farther away from (aphelion) the sun during its annual orbit, approaching 3 million miles nearer to the sun at perihelion than at aphelion. When closest, it receives about 3.5 percent more solar radiation than the annual mean.

Twice each year, on opposite sides of the orbit, the earth's axis of rotation points neither toward or away from the sun. At such times (the vernal and autumnal equinoxes) both hemispheres receive exactly the same number of hours of sunlight.

Because the sun does not sit at the exact center of the ellipse, it takes the earth seven days longer to negotiate the portion of the orbit that lies between the vernal equinox (March 20th) and the autumnal equinox (Septermber 22). Thus, in the northern hemisphere, spring and summer seasons last slightly longer than the autumn and winter seasons.

Currently the earth reaches perihelion at about the time of the winter solstice. The shorter time spent in the winter portion of the orbit and the extra radiation owing to its closer approach to the sun combine to modify northern hemisphere winters.

In about 11,000 years the situation will have reversed. The earth's axis of rotation will have precessed such that it tilts away from the sun on June 21st. Northern hemisphere winters will occur when the earth lies farthest from the sun and spends several additional days traversing the colder portion of the orbit. At that time the decrease in solar radiance, combined with a greater loss of heat from land-mass radiation and reflection, will cause (according to theory) significant increases in glacial growth.

It appears that configurations of orbital eccentricity, tilt and precession combine to cause small but critical changes, not in the amount of sunlight reaching the earth but in the effect of the sunlight as it strikes particular regions of the earth. A significant decrease in the amount of radiation received in northern latitudes during winter apparently will initiate an ice age. Thus, the physical geography of the earth itself seems to play a key role in climate change.

QUESTIONS STILL

Although the cyclical reoccurrence of glaciers implicates the regular variations in the earth's orbit and the axis of rotation, complete consensus does not yet exist. However, most researchers now accept the modified Milankovitch parameters as major influences leading to the development (at least the initiation) of ice ages, and on the rapid fluctuations of glacial growth and decay revealed in ice-core and sea-sediment core analysis.

The astronomical theory cannot explain all of the smaller fluctuations revealed by the ice-core data. Perhaps this should come as no surprise considering the number of forces operating to abet or oppose changes in the earth's climate.

CHAPTER FOURTEEN

THE SUN -- WHERE WEATHER BEGINS

Wherein we pay homage to the sun, the source of energy upon which humans depend for their existence. Additionally, we note the importance of the sun and its effect on people through the ages as revealed in their lore and means of dedication and worship of this marvelous thermonuclear engine. We also note the gradual transformation of the sun from a god to the center of the universe, and ultimately to a relatively small, quite ordinary star amongst billions of others.

"And when the rising sun has first breathed on us with his panting horses, over there the red evening star is lighting his late lamps."
-- Virgil

ENERGY FROM THE RADIANT SUN

Even learned scientists have on occasion advanced the specious argument that "all life on earth depends on energy from the sun." In fact, microbes live under the earth's surface and never feel the sun's warmth. Fantastic creatures thrive on the ocean bottom, at great depths, receiving their heat and nourishment solely from volcanic vents in the sea floor. Some fishes live their lives in cave waters far from the rays of the sun. Scientists now speculate on the possibility that some form of life exists beneath the icy surface of Io, one of Jupiter's moons, where precious little sunlight reaches.

Some scientists have suggested that life on earth derived from incipient life-forms that reached us from outer space, like spoors borne on the interglactic wind. If so, some spoors must have reached the moon as well. If life depended only on sunlight, then life could theoretically exist on the moon -- or possible in free space -- but it does not.

On earth, of course, advanced life-forms, such as primates, require the sun because plants, our basic source of food, once learned photosynthesis -- a process by which they convert light energy into chemical energy, using carbon dioxide from the air and minerals from ground water. Without light from the sun, and water, our fundamental food supply would quickly vanish -- and so would we. Life, in general, has always depended on the constant sun.

Most current forms of earthly life, especially the so-called higher forms of life, evolved under certain ranges of warmth. The sun, of course, provides the initial life-supporting heat but it needs help. It needs the atmosphere and water vapor to transport essential heat and moisture from the equatorial regions to the higher latitudes.

OUR BENEFICENT SUN

In one sense, while existing for several billion years and having traveled many trillions of miles through galactic space, our sun, aside from constancy, has no real history of its own. Except for its internal churning and a slow increase in luminosity over time, the sun that now warms us remains pretty much the same sun that shone upon our human ancestors five million years ago. In another sense, in terms of human occupation of our planet, Man's perception of the sun and its physical and mystical role as our benefactor sculpts a truly fascinating history.

For early Man, danger awaited at every turn and behind every bush. Since he rarely survived long enough to die a natural death, he likely attributed death to some supernatural force and sought means to placate the omnipotent powers that complicated his life. In a life fraught with dangerous and unexpected events -- earthquakes, volcanic eruptions, violent weather, lurking predators -- it would seem logical for ancient Man to seek solace in the constant, orderly progressions of the sun, moon and stars.

To early Man the sky obviously contained tremendous power. The tides resonated with the phases of the moon and the seasons fell into place in concert with the sun and stars. Although few artifacts exist from this early period of human development to indicate what form of worship, if any, they may have employed, it seems reasonable to assume that they gained comfort from the cyclical order and symmetry of the sky. Accordingly they developed myths and ceremonies to acknowledge the source of this never-ending pageantry and the constant, life-sustaining warmth of the sun.

Man's interest in the sun, and his appreciation of its benefits, clearly extends back to the earliest civilizations and probably much further. At some early point in his progress he became aware of his environment and began to notice and give names to the sun, moon and various groups of stars. Eventually he noted that celestial bodies move in orderly and predictable paths, repeating their courses through the heavens each year.

The sun, however, regulated Primitive Man's daily activities. In the beginning, he probably got by easily enough with a day of just two periods -- night and day. As he began to travel farther afield it became necessary to keep a careful eye on the sun, traveling outward while the sun rose and turning back as the sun reached its zenith.

When the need arose to divide the day into smaller increments, he created a sundial by driving a stick upright into the ground. By placing stones at various places at the end of the shadow cast by the stick, he could divide the day into whatever increments he wished. The oldest known sundial (Egyptian) dates to about 1500 B.C. but they no doubt existed long before that time. Some primitive societies still have only sundials to keep time.

THE SUN AS GOD

Each dawn the sun rises at a slightly different spot on the skyline, returning to the initial spot every 365 and a quarter days. Emerging civilizations erected solar observatories where priests, seers and shamans marked the solstices and the equinoxes that signified the changing seasons. Archeologists have found examples of these observatories, ranging from crude circles of wooden posts to elaborate stone temples, over the entire world, from the British Isles through Asia to the rugged peaks of South America's Andes mountains.

Egyptian mathematics did not compare with the Greeks but, as early as 2500 B.C., they had the sun figured out. They built elaborate temple-observatories by which they could determine the exact day the rising sun reached its southernmost position on the horizon -- the occurrence of the winter solstice. Observations of the sun led the Egyptians to develop a useful calendar containing 365 days. Julius Caesar adopted and modified the Egyptian calendar to make the Julian calendar which survived until the Pope Gregory reform in 1582.

Seasons increase in importance with latitude. In the tropics, one season looks pretty much like the next but in the "temperate" latitudes changing seasons herald important changes in the weather. Thus, with increasing distance from the equator it became increasingly necessary for inhabitants to understand and anticipate the seasonal changes.

After agriculture replaced hunting as the main source of food, the sun probably gained status. Prudent people recognized that, without the sun's heat, the soil would yield no bounty. Moreover, the sun's position in the noon-day sky determined the times of sowing and reaping.

The powerful and dependable sun, pursuing its orderly course through the seasons, inspired many early civilizations to attribute to it all authority, law and order. The Sumnerians and the Babylonians had their sun-god, Shamash who drove his chariot through the firmament each day. The ancient Egyptian's sun-god, Ra or Re, ruled the day, traveling through the heavens in a bark accompanied by Maat, the goddess of sunlight. The Persians worshipped Mithra, the god of sun while the Indians had Savitar, the Life-Giver, who became Vivasvat, the Shining God, and finally Prajapati, Lord of all living things.

Later civilizations also personified the sun as god. The Greeks worshipped Helios, the Romans, Sol, and the Indians Surya. In the new world, the Aztecs paid homage to Tonatiuh -- He Who Goes Forth Shining -- while the Inca's raised their sun, Inti, to divine authority.

THE SUN -- CENTER OF THE ANCIENT UNIVERSE

The Greek's sun god, Helios, lived in a radiant place, constructed of gold and ivory and studded with jewels, wherein no shadows dwelt and no darkness ever appeared. The Greeks watched Helios daily drive his sun-chariot through the sky. At the same time, rising through the mists of mythology, the practical

Greeks, gave the world its first geography based primarily on the seasonal change of the sun's noonday elevation.

In the second century B.C., Eratosthenes, acknowledging the spherical shape of the earth, calculated its circumference (to an accuracy of 15 percent) using the shadow cast at high-noon by an obelisk in Alexandria. A century later, Hipparchus of Nicaea, discovered the precession of the equinoxes. He observed that the sun rose higher in the sky during summer. He observed also that the sun's maximum angle, and the average warmth of summer, decreased with distance toward the north. He delineated zones of similar climatic features, (mainly temperature) with *climata* lines drawn parallel to the equator.

Ptolemy, building on the works of Eratosthenes and Hipparchus, improved the earth's geographical grid by introducing equally spaced vertical lines. Ptolomy's vision of the earth, with its east-west "latitude" lines and north-south "longitude" lines, held sway as the definitive world geography until Copernicus.

A Greek philosopher, Aristarchus, first determined the distance from the earth to the moon and the sun using simple geometry. Although his calculations fell substantially short of the true distances, he did recognize a difference in size between the moon and the sun. Consequently, he placed the sun much farther away from earth than the moon and suggested that the sun rather than the earth lay at the center of the universe. Despite the sun's obvious importance, however, most early astronomers continued to place the earth at the center of the universe with rotating spheres overhead holding the sun, the stars and the planets.

After the collapse of the Roman Empire, a period of collective amnesia afflicted the European continent until about 1300. The limited but quite accurate image of the world drawn by the ancient geographers fell prey to ignorance and dogma and eventually became lost to the western world.

During the age of exploration, practical seafarers such as Columbus reintroduced the Ptolemaic version of the universe. Then, in the early 1500s, Copernicus conceived a very different view of the universe. His heliocentric theory, with the sun rather than the earth at the center of the universe, neatly explained the strange motions of the planets and provided a simpler means to calculate the precession of the equinoxes (See Appendix A). Galileo, with his telescope, later confirmed that Copernicus had essentially the correct view of the relative positions of the sun and earth. The earth would never again regain its distinguished position as the center of the universe.

In the mid-1700s, Thomas Wright observed that the Milky Way galaxy (from *galaktos,* the Greek word for milk) consisted of countless millions of stars, including our sun, packed into a thin rotating lens-shaped cluster. Still, he remained convinced that the sun, while only one of many similar stars, occupied the central position within the galaxy -- and thus of the universe.

Lord Kelvin, born William Thompson in 1824, the greatest physicist of the late Victorian age, developed the Kelvin temperature scale and invented absolute zero. He also made a big mistake concerning the sun. Kelvin thought that the sun shines because of frictional heat caused by meteorites and other debris falling into it. He further assumed that the earth had somehow emanated from the sun and, once detached, began to cool, taking just 100 million years to reach its present temperature. For a time Kelvin's prestige, and therefore his opinions, held sway. To the total dismay and consternation of biologists and geologists, and especially evolutionists, Kelvin had wrongly reduced the earth's age from 4.5 billion years to a mere 100 million years.

The sun maintained its exalted position at the center of the galaxy -- and the universe -- for nearly two more centuries. Then, in 1918, Harlow Shapley discovered that the sun actually lies on the outskirts of one arm of the galactic spiral, some 30,000 light-years from the center.

In 1920, Heber Doust Curtis observed other galaxies similar to ours drifting in space millions of light-years from our own Milky Way galaxy. These discoveries not only diminished the sun's status to that of an ordinary star but permanently removed it from its illustrious position as the "center of the universe." Astronomers currently estimate that the Milky Way contains some 150 billion stars, many similar to our sun.

THE RED SUN

Although steadily diminished through the ages in cosmic significance, the sun nevertheless remains vitally important to earthly life. In addition to its life-supporting rays, the sun, with its various aspects, colors and shades, early assumed a primary role as an indicator of weather changes.

Above the rest, the sun who never lies,
Foretells the change of weather in the skies;
For if he rise unwilling to his race,

Clouds on his brow and spots upon his face,
Or if through mists he shoot his sullen beams,
Frugal of light in loose and straggling streams,
Suspect a drizzling day and southern rain,
Fatal to fruits, and flocks, and promised grain.
-- Virgil, *Georgics*

Long before the invention of meteorological instruments, computers or satellites, hunters, shepherds, sailors and farmers learned, by careful observation, to make surprising accurate weather forecasts.

They watched and studied the winds and clouds and gradually amassed a substantial body of lore that indicated impending weather changes. They formulated forecasting rules based on their observations and cast them into rhymes and sayings, which they passed down through the generations. Many have little skill and others apply strictly to locality. Some, such as the universally known

Red sky at morning, sailor take warning;
Red sky at night, sailor's delight.

work everywhere and remain popular because they have a valid meteorological basis.

A red sky at sunset indicates high pressure to the west and continuing fair weather. The sky turns red because, within high-pressure systems, sinking air from the stratosphere prevents vertical motion except very near the ground. Such regions often trap large quantities of dust, smoke, pollen, and other pollutants in the lower few thousand feet. Light from the setting sun, having a longer path through the polluted atmosphere, slows down a little and shifts into the red part of the visible spectrum. Conversely, a red sunrise indicates high pressure to the east and thus, very likely, a storm approaching from the west.

Refraction of sunlight through the ice crystals of high cirrus clouds produces rings or halos around the moon or sun. The appearance of halos signifies an approaching storm. A considerable amount of weather lore, some quite reliable, has accumulated around the various corona/sun-halo phenomena.

Ring around the moon, rain by noon;
Ring around the sun, rain before night is done.

Moreover, rings or halos increase in size as the storm draws near and clouds lower. Thus,

The bigger the ring, the nearer the wet.

Although the moon also has a reputation for influence over the rain and clouds, the sun remains always the first authority.

COLORS OF THE ATMOSPHERE

Thermonuclear fusion within the sun's core generates the intense energy that constantly bathes the earth. The sun transmits its energy to the earth via electromagnetic waves. Visible light, that which the human eye can discern, composes 37 percent of the electromagnetic spectrum. Shorter-wave ultra-violet rays make up 12 percent and longer infra-red rays occupy 45 percent of the total spectrum. Extremely long (radio) and extremely short (gamma) waves make up the remaining six percent.

Of the sun's electromagnetic energy reaching the earth, the upper atmosphere reflects 40 percent and absorbs 15 percent. The remaining 45 percent penetrates to lower levels where it becomes further reflected, absorbed by cloud or smoke or reaches the earth unimpeded. Those rays that strike solid objects become partially absorbed and partially reflected by the object. The portion absorbed becomes converted to heat and re-radiated into the atmosphere. The remaining portion becomes reflected or refracted in certain wavelengths by the fine grains of pigment composing the surface, and discerned by the human eye as the color of the object.

In general, the atmosphere absorbs the bulk of the longer and shorter wavelengths. Our eyes evolved to gather those rays of the electromagnetic spectrum that most efficiently penetrate the atmosphere. Owing to the limited amount of ultraviolet or infrared radiation reaching the earth's surface, an eye attuned to those wavelengths could not see as well as our eyes do.

The interaction of sunlight with the various gases and pollutants that constitute the atmosphere produces a variety of colorful phenomena. Sunlight in the visible portion of the spectrum passing through a densely polluted atmosphere produces the brilliant red or orange sunrises and sunsets. The greater the degree of pollution, the greater the intensity of red.

Sunlight scattered by gas molecules that compose the air generates the ubiquitous blue of the sky. As observed by astronauts, the sky grows successively dark with height since fewer molecules of gas exist in the upper reaches of the atmosphere. The blue sky pales when the air contains a lot of dust and changes to white when tiny ice crystals, growing in the stratosphere, produce a thin veil of cirrostratus.

Clouds range in color from dazzling white to dull gray to nearly pure black. Sunlight and reflection from other clouds provides the primary illumination. The intensity depends on several factors but mainly on the relative positions of the sun and the observer. Depending on the observer's position, a cumulus cloud growing in the bright afternoon sunshine might appear bright white or a dark gray.

Depending again on the relative positions of the sun and the observer, refraction and defraction of sunlight through water drops may produce a rainbow. Sometimes secondary and even tertiary rainbows appear. The early Greeks knew the rainbow as the goddess, Iris, messenger of the gods, who used her rainbow as a highway in the sky to bring news and deliver messages - - and also to draw water into the clouds.

CORONAS, HALOS AND OTHER OPTICAL MARVELS

When sunlight (or moonlight) shines through a fairly thin low cloud layer, the light rays bend slightly as they pass through the water drops and produce a faint disk of color, called a corona. Blue appears near the center and a brownish red around the outside of the disk.

Many types of colored or whitish rings, arcs and halos appear about the sun or moon when their light shines through an ice crystal cloud, or in a sky filled with falling ice crystals. Some halos, produced by refraction of light by the crystals, exhibit prismatic coloration while those produced by reflection from the crystal faces exhibit only a whitish luminosity. In a colored halo, the red occurs nearest the sun or moon, as opposed to the corona where the red appears in the exterior ring.

The type of phenomena -- sun dogs, sun crosses, light pillars and so forth -- depends on the shape, orientation and motion of the ice crystals forming the cloud and the angle of the sun. Because of the multitude of possible combinations, a large variety of halos can, theoretically, appear. Some theoretically possible halo phenomena have yet to be observed while others, such as the Hevelian halo, have been reported but not yet theoretically explained.

When the sky contains a layer of hexagonal (six-sided) shaped ice crystals of uniform size, falling with random orientations, a halo may appear about the sun (or moon). The halo of 22° (the angle between the light source and the outer ring of the halo) occurs most frequently, with the parhelia or parselanae a poor second. Sun pillars, the circumscribed halo, the circumzenith arc, the halo of 46°, the parhelic circle, the arcs of Lowitz and sun crosses occur less frequently in that order. Our ancient ancestors no doubt held these apparitions in great awe and recognized them as harbingers of changing weather.

THE SUN AND CLIMATE

Episodes of glaciation have periodically devastated earthly life over the past few million years. Some 65 million years ago, after the Cretaceous/ Tertiary catastrophe, the earth began to cool rapidly. About 35 million years ago, changes in shape, size and location of the continents combined to produce a colder earth with ice forming near the poles.

Fifteen million years ago, glaciers formed in Antarctica. Ten million years ago, small glaciers appeared on mountains in the higher latitudes of North America. Seven million years ago the great northern-hemisphere ice sheet began to grow and two and one-half million years ago a sheet of ice spread over Greenland.

Over the last 500 thousand years, Earth has endured at least four periods of extreme glaciation during which walls of ice spread into the northern United States and Europe. Each has lasted some 100 thousand years, interrupted only by brief, 20,000 year warm periods.

Although some researchers have tried to implicate changes in the sun's solar radiation as the cause of Pleistocene glaciation, they have yet to gather conclusive evidence of significant long-term increases or decreases in the sun's intensity. According to some investigators, instruments on the ACRIM satellite have indicated an increase of some 0.036 percent in solar radiation received at the edge of our atmosphere during the last decade. Other investigators translate the data differently and see a decrease in radiation rather than an increase.

While an increase of 0.036 percent might have a significant effect on the earth's climate, greenhouse gas pollution currently exerts two to three times that influence on climate and effectively masks changes from small oscillations in solar intensity. If, however, the sun's luminosity continued to increase at the rate of 0.036 percent per decade, it could supplement the current global warming trend.

In general, most climatic investigators believe that variations in earthly features -- continental drift, mountain building and changes in earth-sun aspects (tilt and wobble) -- probably play a larger role in climate than variations in solar intensity. Long-term changes in intensity owing to orbital variations or precession of the axis of rotation may produce extended changes in weather and thus the climate.

Instruments on satellites track the amount of solar energy reaching the earth and have measured ebbs and surges associated with the well-known 11-year sunspot cycle. At the peak of a sunspot cycle, hundreds of dark spots blemish the surface of the sun while bright regions pour out and extra 0.10 percent radiation. Changes in the sun's output during sunspot cycles affect the earth but have little effect on the overall climate -- although some evidence exists to correlate the Little Ice Age that occurred in Europe between 1650 and 1700 AD with an extended period of very low sunspot activity.

Studies of stars similar to the sun indicate that the early sun produced only 70 to 80 percent of the present rate of energy output -- a figure that has steadily increased since that time. If so, the young earth would have received much less solar radiation than it does today and, according to calculations, the temperature of the planet today should exceed that of the Precambrian by some 10 to 15 degrees (C). Based on evidence from the rock record, however, paleoclimatologists think that 600 million years ago the atmosphere contained much more carbon dioxide and the Precambrian climate did not differ much from our present climate.

THE SUN AND ATMOSPHERIC CHEMISTRY

The sun affects weather in less obvious ways than just heating the earth's surface. Variations in energy delivered to the earth's atmosphere by solar radiation produces short-term variations in the global circulation by causing chemical changes in the atmosphere.

A few times each decade, the sun increases its output significantly. This leads to a large increase in atmospheric ionization which some researchers have associated with climate and weather changes. Ionization leads to a dramatic increase in the production of ice crystals in the upper atmosphere which gradually fall into the lower atmosphere. When they fall into existing clouds they act to increase precipitation and latent heat release, cyclone intensity, and ultimately affect the general circulation.

Measurements of carbon isotopes in sediment cores suggest that the atmosphere may respond to long-term solar variations in ways that could contribute to climate changes as great as those produced by increases in various greenhouse gases.

Apparently changes in the sun's ultraviolet radiation output may cause changes in the ozone content of the upper atmosphere. Although the subject generates considerable debate, some computer simulations indicate that changes in the upper atmosphere slowly translate downward into the weather sphere. We still have much to learn concerning the relationship between the sun and our atmosphere.

CHAPTER FIFTEEN

THE HISTORY OF AIR

Wherein we note the uneasy relationship that exists between humans and the moving air (wind). Wind, a ubiquitous paradox -- a vital necessity and a potentially dangerous nuisance -- derives from the generally beneficial atmospheric movements that carry the life-giving heat and moisture from the balmy tropical regions to less congenial lands to the north and south. From the beginning, Man has utilized the wind for his benefit. But the gods have tempered this beneficence with many harsh winds that blow little but ill.

"The wind, as moving air, touches us directly, sometimes brutally."
-- Lyall Watson

VISUALIZING THE UNSEEABLE

Until the scientists of the early civilizations began to investigate the physical nature of the earth, the concept of air probably had little meaning. Air in itself has no taste or smell and, unless colored by smoke, dust or other aerosols, remains invisible to the eye.

Yet, humans have always possessed at least a vague awareness that *something* surrounded them. Moreover, that something, while undetectable by ordinary senses, revealed its presence in interesting, often provoking, and occasionally frightening, ways.

Something rushed through the trees making haunting, aeolian tones, rustling leaves and bending blades of grass. Something caused smoke from the campfire to swirl about and smart the eyes. Something transported the scent of flowers or the smell of approaching rain, conveyed the sound of distant thunder, lifted the birds and carried the humming insects.

GODS OF THE WIND

The Greek philosopher, Anaximander, gave us the first recorded scientific definition of wind. He realized that pure air, while having no taste or smell, did have substance because he could feel it when it moved. He called the wind a "flowing of air." The American Meteorological Society, attempting to improve this definition, calls wind "air in motion relative to the earth." When Anaximander's colleague, Anaximenes, noticed that clouds formed from air, He concluded (correctly) that air, when rarefied by the heat of the sun, rises to produce wind.

The ancient Greeks knew that air, in the guise of wind, existed and they associated certain types of weather with certain prevailing winds. Hesiod, the ninth century B.C. Greek poet and philosopher -- possibly the first man in Greece to contrive an explanation for the world, the sky, the gods and mankind itself -- harbored a profound hatred for the northeast wind.

. . . as the breath of the north-easter from Thrace bloweth on the wide sea and stirreth it, and earth and wood bellow aloud. Many an oak of lofty foliage and many a stout pine in the mountain glens doth his onset bring low to the bounteous earth, and all the unnumbered forest crieth aloud, and the wild beast shudder and set their tails between their legs, even they whose hide is covered with hair. Yea, even through these, shaggy-breasted though they are, he bloweth with chill breath. Through the hide of the ox he bloweth, and it stayeth him not, and through the thin-haired goat: but nowise through the sheep doth the might of Boreas blow because of their abundant wool. But he maketh the old man bent.

Hippocrates, the father of medicine, placed great emphasis on the effect wind has on human health and comfort. He urged physicians, upon arrival at an unfamiliar town, to become acquainted with the prevailing hot and cold winds, believing they greatly influenced human health.

Yet, even as the Greek philosophers accumulated knowledge of the earth and skies, they didn't forget their gods. The Greek gods, ruled by Zeus, god of the heavens, lived in Olympus. To enter Olympus, the gods passed through a great gate of clouds guarded by the Seasons. Zeus permitted no rain, snow, wind or even clouds to inconvenience those who dwelt there. In this cloudless abode, suffused with sunshine, the gods lived, feasting on ambrosia and nectar and listening to Apollo's lyre.

Considering the prevailing universal presence of weather and its impact on the lives of humans, it comes as little surprise to find the greatest of the Greek gods, Zeus himself, Lord of the Sky, the Rain-god, the Cloud-gatherer, he who wielded the awful thunderbolt, in control of the weather.

Strangely, however, Zeus, sometimes lost control. At one time he appointed Aeolis his "keeper of the winds," to use them as he would. Aeolis, not an actual god, lived on earth on the island of Aeolia where he served as viceroy to the four chief winds, Boreas, the north wind, Eurus, the east wind, Notus, the south wind and Zephyr, the west wind of spring.

Aeolis kept the adverse winds tied tightly in a leather bag. Unfortunately, in a moment of carelessness, he left the bag in the care of Odysseus. One night, while Odysseus slept, his companions opened the bag out of curiosity and released all the adverse winds -- with subsequent dire consequences.

The octagonal Tower of the Winds, commissioned by Julius Ceasar and erected in Athens in the first century B.C., further illustrates the awe and appreciation ancient people held for the omnipresent wind.

Andronikos, who designed and built the tower, decorated each side with a deity dressed appropriately for the weather associated with the wind that blew from that direction -- Boreas (N), Kaikias (NE), Apeliotes (E), Euros (SE), Notos (S), Ips (SW), Zephyros (W) and Skiiron (NW).

WINDS OF THE LAND

Each region, each valley and each town has its own set of vexing winds, many of which have become legendary.

Boreus, the north wind, renowned for its irksome disruptiveness and rarely appreciated, has been personalized in many localities. The bora (Italy and Yugoslavia), the bise (Switzerland and France), the buran and the purga (Russia), the mistral (France and Spain), the tramontana (Italy and Corsica), the gregale (Greece), the harmattan (northwest Africa) and the tehauntepecer (U.S. and Mexico) have gained distinction for reliability, persistence and violence.

The Harmattan blows southward out of the Sahara desert toward the coast. When this very, very dry dusty wind reaches the African coast it wilts vegetation and has been known to cause human skin to peel off. The Australians have a similar wind they call the Brickfielder.

A hot, dry desert wind, called the Santa Ana, blows, sometimes with great force, from the deserts northeast of the Sierra Nevada into the valleys and coastal areas of southern California. It frequently carries large amounts of dust and, when it comes in spring, may do great damage to fruit trees.

Tehauntepecers originate in Canada. They zoom through the Midwest shattering minimum temperature records, sail across the Gulf of Mexico and rush into the Pacific Ocean through the Tehauntepec isthmus between the Mexican and Guatemalan mountains. Mariners in the tropical Pacific Ocean notice the effects of these violent outbreaks 100 miles west of Mexico.

Tehauntepecers come and go within a few days but the northwestern seistan blows through Afghanistan and eastern Iran all summer long. This fierce "wind of 120 days," once clocked at over 70 miles per hour, carries sand and dust that grind away buildings and choke water supplies. Buildings in regions affected by the seistan have no openings on the windward side, attesting to the frequency and ravaging force of this unrelenting wind.

Except in the tropics, where soft, gentle trade winds ply, an east wind rarely pleases. North winds may penetrate and freeze the bone, but east winds provide a wide variety of misery. Depending on their origin, they may bring a withering dryness or a damp, cloudy cold that erodes the spirit. Even in the balmy southeastern U.S., they often bring dismal weather conditions.

Since biblical times, residents of the near-east have dreaded the east wind.

And, behold, seven thin ears, and blasted with the east wind, came up.
  --Genesis xii. 6.

When the east wind toucheth it, it shall wither.
  -- Ezekiel, xvii. 10.

The east wind brought the locusts.
-- Exodus x. 13.

The greatest wind damage and heaviest snowfalls along the northeast coast of the United States occur with east winds. The violent Nor'easter, a wind that often blows from the northeast into the New England and Maritime Provinces between September and April, generates large waves which crash on shore washing away beaches, dunes, and houses.

South winds generally behave better than north or east winds. The chinook blowing northward along on the eastern side (front range) of the Rocky Mountains brings temporary relief from the cold of winter. Chinooks can raise temperatures 20 degrees in minutes and melt a foot of snow in a few hours. At Havre, Montana, a chinook once raised the temperature from 11 degrees to 42 degrees in three minutes.

Certain south winds, however, rival their northern counterparts in malefic oppressiveness. The khamsin, a hot, corrosive, sand-laden south wind, frequents Egypt and the Red Sea during the spring. This dreaded southeast wind, known also as the Sirocco in Arabia, the Chergui in Algeria, the Chili in Tunisia, the Ghibli in Libya, the Sharav in Israel and the Shamal in Iraq, continues for days during which time it "blows away all gaiety and spirit, extinguishes all vivacity, and bestows a degree of lassitude, both to the body and the mind, that renders natives and visitors alike absolutely incapable of performing their usual functions."

Occasionally these desert windstorms travel across the Mediterranean from the Sahara. The air loses dust on its passage over the sea but gathers much moisture because of its high temperature. It reaches Malta, Sicily, and southern Italy as a very hot, humid, enervating wind, and causes "langour and mental debility" to residents of southern Europe. A similar wind, the leveche, blows across the Strait of Gibraltar from Africa causing heat waves in Spain.

WINDS OF THE SEA

By 3000 BC, substantial sea-going ships plied the Mediterranean sea and by 1800 BC, the Minoans on Crete controlled a vast maritime trade that extended throughout the Mediterranean and into the Atlantic ocean. Sailors, who identified sailing directions with prevailing winds, became the worlds best weather observers and forecasters. Their very lives depended upon their skill in detecting changes in the weather and taking appropriate action. Since they had no instruments to measure wind, they developed crude means to gauge the wind speed, based on its effect on the sea and on ships.

In the days of exploration, a lack of wind often presented a worse problem than too much wind. In the middle of the 15th century when the great voyages of discovery began, mariners regarded the open ocean with fear and dread. Of the many dangerous encounters with the elements at sea, the one least expected and most dreaded, turned out to be a total lack of wind -- the infamous doldrums.

Near the equator, air warmed by the heated ocean rises to form a line of thunderstorms thousands of miles long across the Atlantic and Pacific oceans. The rising air creates a vacuum at the ocean surface. Air flows into the vacuum from the northeast and southeast of the thunderstorm line but, as it nears the line, it also begins to rise. This creates a zone of calm or baffling winds. Unless the ships captain sailed carefully it could take him a month to traverse the zone.

A second region of near calm winds occurs near the center of the sub-tropical high pressure cells, which lie 30 to 35 degrees north and south of the equator in the Atlantic and Pacific oceans. The sub-tropical high separates the easterly trades from the westerly winds of the temperate latitudes. In the center, air sinks and warms, creating clear skies and weeks of dull enervating heat and calm winds.

In the early 19th century, Admiral Beaufort of the British Navy, formalized the descriptions of wind force currently used by sailors into a standard scale that described the effects of various wind speeds on "a well conditioned man-of-war, under all sail." The Beaufort Scale, in modified and modernized form, remains with us today (see Appendix A). In its current form it equates the Beaufort Force (Beaufort number) with wind speed and a description of the wind (calm, light, fresh etc.) with the visible effects of its exertion on land objects or water surfaces.

POETRY IN THE WIND

Who has seen the wind
Neither you nor I
But when the trees bow down their heads
The wind is passing by
    --Cristina Rossetti

When the wind is in the east,
It is neither good for man nor beast.
When the wind is in the west,
The weather is always best.
    -- Old Weather sayin'

The north wind doth blow
And we shall have snow
    -- Denham

How thy garments are warm, when He quieteth the earth by the south
wind.
    -- Job xxxvii. 17

The south wind warms the aged.
    -- old weather sayin'

And a good south wind sprung up behind;
The Albatross did follow,
And every day, for food or play,
Came to the mariner's hollo!
    -- Samuel T. Coleridge

SHAKESPEAREAN WINDS

Therefore the winds have sucked up from the sea
Contagious fogs, which, falling in the land,
Have every pelting river made so proud,
That they have overborne their continents.

--Shakespeare, *"Midsummer Night's Dream."*

And more inconstant than the wind, who woos
Even now the frozen bosom of the north;
And being angered, puffs away from thence,
Turning his face to the dew-dropping south.
  -- Shakespeare, *Romeo and Juliet*

. . . the southern wind
Doth play the trumpet to his purposes,
And by his hollow whistling in the leaves
Foretells a tempest and a blustering day.
  -- Shakespeare, *King Henry IV*

Shakespeare employed a wide range of meteorological metaphor. He engaged the wind to produce images of speed, with Oberon urging, "go swifter than the wind," and of freedom, with Prospero promising, "thou shalt be free as the mountain wind." He effectively used storms at sea in the *Tempest, Othello* and *Pericles.* and, in *Troilus and Cressida,* even introduced a waterspout. In *King Lear,* he generated the famous gale that cracked its cheeks.

In *King Henry* he used the ominous portent of a fierce storm to prepare his audience for the violent battle Henry must soon fight. In this case, however, Shakespeare may have mixed his metaphors -- or at least rebuffed convention.

The Roman poet, Ovid, precisely defined the four cardinal winds in the first century AD. His personification guided most Medieval and Renaissance poets, artists and writers in their metaphoric applications of the wind and weather. In Ovid's eye, the *north* wind, Boreas, had the trumpet.

Ovid represented Boreas as an old man with flowing gray locks blowing through his conch-shell trumpet. Strong in body and harsh in disposition -- Shakespeare called him "that ruffian Boreas" -- he personified winter and the humour of middle-age.

Boreas' brother, Zephyrus, represented the west wind. In his youth, Zephyrus also raged about, generating savage and baleful winds. But, under the influence of Chloris, the goddess of spring, he mellowed. Ovid pictured him, in his more amiable guise, as a genteel, almost effeminate, god sailing by with his cloak filled with flowers. Zephrus identifies with water and old-age.

Ovid portrayed Eurus, the east wind as a dark-complexioned old man with a fierce countenance, exuding gloom and the bilious humour generally associated with most east winds.

The south wind, Notus or Auster, associated with youth and spring, flew by wrapped in a cloud. Ovid saw him as a young man with water streaming down his hair, carrying an inverted jar from which he spilled rain over Greece and Rome.

In Shakespeare's England, however, the south wind usually heralds the approach of yet another storm blowing in from the North Atlantic. And who's to argue if Shakespeare wanted to give him a trumpet.

Ovid also defined the ancillary winds. Skiron, who blew from the northwest, appeared as an old, intemperate man, bearing a fire-pot of burning coals. Talk about harsh weather! Kaikias, generally portrayed as a stern older man bearing a shield covered in hailstones or ripe autumn olives, ushered in cold and rain from the northeast. Lips, a serious young man blew gusty in from the southwest while the young Apeliotes bore gentle rain and ripe fruit on the southeast wind.

A FINAL WORD ON WIND

This very gentle, poetic, rather archaic view of wind and air defined the theme for the 6th international design competition held by the Japan Design Foundation in Osaka, Japan, during the summer of 1993.

The wind is the stream of air which surrounds the earth, and it creates drama. Wind, as one of the four elements (earth, water, fire, and air) of our planet, has been nurturing the imagination of mankind since time began. Wind is a form of energy to turn windmills and move vessels; man now rides the wind to fly all around the world. Wind gently shakes flowers, makes a calm forest resound with a natural symphony; produces an environment friendly to man. The simple sound of a reed pipe moves the heart and Bach's solemn organ music would not have come into being without wind.

-- Kaze: Wind, Air -- beautiful ambiance.

While often refreshing and essentially beneficial, wind may wreck havoc when it mutates from a gentle zephyr to a raging 150-mile-per-hour hurricane. Thus, the wind, a ubiquitous paradox, at once a vital necessity and a potentially dangerous nuisance, remains always in our consciousness.

Weather-wise, and comfort-wise, this Old Weather Sayin' says it all.

No weather is ill,
If the wind be still.

APPENDIX A

THE BEAUFORT WIND SCALE FOR USE ON LAND

Beaufort Force	Description	Specification on Land	Speed
0	Calm	Smoke rises vertically	Less than 1
1	Light Air	Direction of wind shown by smoke drift but not by wind vane	1 - 3
2	Light Breeze	Wind felt on face, leaves rustle, ordinary wind vane moved by wind	4 - 7
3	Gentle Breeze	Leaves and small twigs in constant motion, wind vane moved by wind	8 - 12
4	Moderate Breeze	Wind raises dust and loose paper, small branches move	13 - 18
5	Fresh Breeze	Small trees in leaf start to sway, crested wavelets on inland waters	19 - 24
6	Strong Breeze	Large branches in motion, whistling in telegraph wires, umbrellas used with difficulty	25 - 31
7	Near Gale	Whole trees in motion, inconvenient to walk against wind	32 - 38
8	Gale	Twigs break from trees, difficult to walk	39 - 46
9	Strong Gale	Slight structural damage occurs, chimney pots and slates removed	47 - 54
10	Storm	Trees uprooted, considerable damage occurs	55 - 63
11	Violent storm	Widespread damage	64 - 73
12	Hurricane	Widespread damage	>74

CHAPTER SIXTEEN

METEOROSENSITIVITY AND OTHER FOLK LORE

Wherein we look at some interesting facets of weather lore -- folk lore, proverbs, weather sayin's, animal forecasters, almanacs, and meteoro-sensitive people who forecast changes in the weather with their bones

Hark how the chairs and tables crack
Old Betty's bones are on the rack.
-- Old English Ditty

BIOTROPIC WEATHER

We don't know who Betty was but many people can certainly empathize with her. She probably suffered from arthritis. When the tables and chairs began to crack, indicating an increase in humidity (and probably a change in the weather), poor Betty began to "feel it in her bones."

Although, to a degree, everyone reacts to major changes in temperature, humidity and other weather parameters, meteorosensitives like Betty sense these changes at a much higher level of perceptivity. Usually they suffer from a degenerative disease or orthopedic injury that becomes aggravated when atmospheric conditions change. Thus, they attune to impending weather changes long before they become obvious to the average person. They can, in a sense, predict the weather.

Interest by scientists and doctors in the phenomena of meterosensitivity predates Hyppocrates. References to aches and pains caused by environmental conditions reach back to medical archives from ancient Egypt and Greece and continue through the present.

Empirical evidence indicates a positive correlation between meteorosensitives and the (more or less) orderly progression of weather events. In a recent publication, two university professors wrote a detailed account about a person who claimed to suffer increased pain in the "lateral cutaneous branch of his subcostal neuron" several days before it rained. When the doctors compared occurrences of pain to rainy days, the man's back proved to be an excellent five-day forecaster for rain, fog or mist.

Although such "evidence" usually exists in the form of anecdotes, some rigorous studies have validated the phenomena. In 1877 doctor S. Weir Mitchell published a detailed account of a Civil War Captain who had lost a leg in the conflict but experienced phantom pain in the missing leg when storms approached.

Another recent study revealed that individuals may react to a given atmospheric change the same way each time but rarely do two individuals have the same reaction. In this experiment, a sudden temperature drop caused various aches and pains in 10 percent of a group of volunteers, exhilarated another 10 percent, but had no affect on the remaining 80 percent.

Possibly the causes of pain and discomfort from weather changes go deeper than previously thought. One theory suggests that, since our bodies run on electricity, we react to electromotive forces generated during thunderstorms. Collections of ions generated during storms produce such phenomena as Saint Elmo's Fire and Ball Lightning as well as ordinary lightning strikes. Possibly vagrant electrical forces floating around in the air during thunderstorms cause spurious reactions in the neurons of a meteorosensitive individual.

METEOROLOGICAL MYTHOLOGY

When it thunders in the day of the moon's disappearance,
the crops will prosper and the market will be steady.
-- adage of the Babylonian priest, Asaridu

The earliest civilizations attributed the erratic nature of weather to their gods. Yet, clay tablets from ancient Babylon reveal samples of weather lore based on observation rather than superstition and imagination. Evidently weather forecasting -- the world's first science -- developed coincidentally with the advance of civilization.

The Ionians and Greeks also related weather (and all natural phenomena) to their gods. Zeus, cleaved the sky with bolts of lightning followed by thunder and the brightly-colored rainbow of Iris. Still, curiosity prevailed. Philosophers and men of science continued to make objective investigations into natural phenomena.

Then as now, most people just wanted to know tomorrow's weather. To satisfy this popular demand, the Greek philosopher, Theophrastus, gathered the cumulative store of ancient observation and lore into one volume, "The Book of Signs." Later, the Greek poet, Aratus, wove these rules into popular verses and proverbs. Many, including the well-known "Red sky in the morning" rhyme, survive to this very day.

LORE AND MORE LORE

Lore and wisdom often consort. It seems reasonable to assume that those most concerned with the seasons, and their suitability for agriculture, husbandry or fishing, would have made the earliest attempts at weather guessing. No doubt they carefully watched the winter and early spring weather and combined it with prior experience, a little superstition and a fair reliance upon fortune to determine the chances of a good harvest.

In some instances, notably Candlemas Day and the early part of February in general, French, Scotch, and English weather sayings agree quite well. It appears that English farmers believed a cold winter augured a bountiful harvest, and a warm Christmas could do nothing but harm.

No statistical evidence would convince the mediaeval peasant that certain saints' days did not exerted a special influence on the weather. Some still express belief in St. Swithin and St. Valentine as weather prophets. On the other hand, even should these venerable saints fail to make an accurate forecast, their guidance no doubt matched that provided by modern almanacs.

Although many old weather sayings fail the test of verification, they still have historical interest. They show us what kind of weather our forefathers thought most useful in their times. Some also indicate changes in climate over the last two centuries. Many display a morose sense of humor.

Dirty days hath September,
April, June and November;
From January up to May,
The rain it raineth every day.
All the rest have thirty-one,
Without a blessed gleam of sun;
And if any of them had two-and-thirty,
They'd be just as wet and twice as dirty.

Perverse laments such as this no doubt helped beleaguered Maine residents through their long gloomy winters.

SEASONS

Spring. Slippy, drippy, nippy.
Summer. Showery, flowery, bowery.
Autumn. Hoppy, croppy, poppy.
Winter. Wheezy, sneezy, breezy.
   -- Attributed to Sydney Smith.

Sydney Smith cleverly breaks the standard seasons into recognizable months by using descriptive terms often associated with them (showers, in April; flowers, in May). This may work in the so-called "Temperate Zone" where one normally finds four distinct, recognizable seasons. It works less well in other parts of the world, where seasons only vaguely resemble the traditional four.

Tropical regions have just two distinguishable seasons -- wet and the dry. Southeast Asia has three -- cold, hot, and wet (monsoonal). The far northern regions have, practically speaking, only two seasons -- a long cold winter and a short warm summer. Spring and fall, if even noticed, last about one month each.

Even within the United States, depending on location and elevation, wide variations in expected weather occur within a given season. Residents of

Havre, Montana, (48 degrees north and 2584 feet above sea level) endure a winter at least six months long while folks in Miami, Florida, bask in an equally long summer.

Our habit of naming the seasons according to the sun's equinoxes and solstices may put them out of whack with their descriptive meanings. Astronomically, April falls in early-spring but, in reality, a lot of winter weather occurs in April. Moreover, as we have learned, in a few thousand years April will fall in mid-winter.

Europeans traditionally recognize May Day as the boundary between winter and summer. The warm days and the riotous flowering of nature confirm the end of winter and afford an occasion for celebration and feasting.

The ancient Celts of Europe recognized only two seasons. Summer began on May Day, and winter began on what we now call Halloween. May Day, which they called "Beltine," or "bright fire," heralded the season of open pasturing. They sent their flocks and herds to the uplands for the summer and didn't bring them back until the first of November.

Sir Frances Bacon put it this way.

"It is sufficiently agreed that all things change, and that nothing really disappears, but that the sum of matter remains the same."

He expressed this same feeling of continuity in many of his weather sayings.

"A serene autumn denotes a windy winter; a windy winter, a rainy spring; a rainy spring, a serene summer; a serene summer, a windy autumn, so that the air on a balance is seldom debtor to itself."

Bacon noted that "Nature is often hidden, sometimes overcome, seldom extinguished." To put it in other words, changes occur and very little remains constant, yet, a balance exists in the local climate that eventually returns conditions to normal -- or nearly so.

SPRING

Farmers paid close attention to spring because it foretold the weather for the rest of the season or, in some cases, the remainder of the year. The farmer, of course, kept his eye always to the harvest.

A late spring
Is a great bless-ing.

A dry spring, rainy summer.

A wet spring, a dry harvest.

SUMMER

Happy are the fields that receive summer rain.

Midsummer rain spoils hay and grain.

Generally a moist and cool summer portends a hard winter.

A hot and dry summer . . . especially if the heat and drought extend far into September, portend an open beginning of winter, and cold to succeed towards the latter part of the winter and beginning of spring.

FALL

When the days begin to lengthen,
The cold begins to strengthen.

A wet fall indicates a cold and early winter.

A fair and dry autumn brings in always a windy winter.

Clear autumn, windy winter;
Warm autumn, long winter.

WINTER

When there is a spring in the winter, or a winter in the spring, the year is never good.

A warm and open winter portends a hot and dry summer.

Who doffs his coat on a winter's day,
Will gladly put it on in May.

MONTHLY MYTHS

Most lore seems to anticipate the consequences of abnormal weather. If the weather hews closely to the average, the farmer can expect a good harvest. If it veers much from the average, the farmer can expect a poor harvest.

The farmer watches the critical months of January through May with well deserved scrutiny. These months reputedly define the conditions for the coming summer and fall. He also closely watches the months of September through November for they foretell the winter weather -- which portends the spring weather which portends the summer weather.

JANUARY

January, the blackest month, provides but little comfort. One dare not hope for a warm January, however, because that portends a cold spring -- which adversely affects all kinds of agricultural activities. A cold January, however, portends a good harvest. Perforce, the hapless peasant must endure the cold weather with as much good cheer as he can muster.

When oak trees bend with snow in January, good crops may be expected.

If January calends be summerly gay,
It will be winterly weather till the calends of May.

The first three days of January rule the coming three months.

If St. Paul's Day (25th) be faire and cleare,
It doth betide a happy year;
But if by chance it then should rain,
It will make deare all kinds of graine;
And if ye clouds make dark ye sky,
Then neate and fowles this yeare shall die;
If blustering winds do blow aloft,
Then wars shall trouble ye realm full oft.

FEBRUARY

Our popular "Groundhog Day" has its roots in Mediaeval Europe. In Germany, the badger, equally as sensitive as our groundhog, peeped out of his hole on Candlemas Day. If he found snow he emerged from his hole, but if he saw the sun shining he retreated back into his hole.

While no statistical evidence exists to support this popular belief, Groundhog Day could have some meteorological basis. Weather frequently comes in cycles producing persistent periods of fair or stormy weather. A cold bright day in early February could portend an extended winter.

When the groundhog peeks out of his hole he doesn't care about his shadow. He notices that the weather, after considering the windchill factor and everything, is way too cold. He therefore decides to wait a few more weeks before venturing out. On the other hand, a damp cloudy February day might not be so cold, in which case the groundhog gambles that winter has gone and sallies forth.

In Spain,

When it rains at Candlemas, the cold is over.

In France,

On the eve of Candlemas Day,
Winter gets stronger or passes away.

In Scotland,

If Candlemas Day be fair and clear,
There'll be twa [two] winters in the year.

In England,

As far as the sun shines in on Candlemas Day,
So far will the snow blow in May.

MARCH

"March comes in like a lion and goes out like a lamb," says the sayin'. True, March weather usually ends better than it begins. As far as it's gentle behavior near the end, however, depends a lot on where you live. Only a blind optimist would put much faith in a weather sayin' that predicts lamb-like weather in places like, say, Cut Bank, Montana, where blizzards and sub-freezing temperatures continue well into May.

In some lands, notably western Europe, unusually stormy weather frequently occurs during the last three days of March to punish mortals who would fail to keep their promises.

Once, on a severely cold March day in Spain, a shepherd tried vainly to find a place to shelter his herd of sheep from the fierce wind. In desperation, fearing that he would lose his flock, he appealed to March. If March would temper the wind, he would to pay a lamb in return.

March obliged but the shepherd then refused to pay the lamb. March, in furious revenge, extended his blustery sway by borrowing three days from April. During these three days, March caused even more fierce winds to blow, thus suitably punishing the duplicitous shepherd. The fable says nothing of the suffering endured by shepherd's hapless neighbors who had to share his punishment. Perhaps they had their own transgressions to atone for.

Judging from the lore, similar happenings have occurred in England and Scotland as well.

March borrowit from April
Three days, and they were ill:
The first was frost, the second was snaw,
The third was cauld as ever't could blaw

The story goes slightly different in Greece. Once, on the island of
Kythnos, an old woman mistook March for a summer month. This so angered
March that he borrowed a day from his brother, February, and froze her and
her flocks to death.
    In general, the farmer prefers a dry March.

A bushel of March dust is a thing
Worth the ransom of a king.

A wet March makes a sad harvest.

March damp and warm
Will do the farmer much harm.

APRIL

April, April,
Laugh thy girlish laugh,
Then, the moment after,
Weep thy girlish tears!
    -- Sir Wm. Watson

"April showers bring May flowers." This happy alliance of rhyme, general
accuracy and optimism expresses the very basis of weather lore -- the
expectation that what has past will recur.
    Crops that grow in a given region do so because they require the climate
that exists there. If a crop requires April rain, then that crop grows where it
rains in April. Thus, the farmer expects, and usually gets, April showers. If
April fails to produce showers, the farmer suffers.

In April each drop counts for a thousand.

April rain is worth David's chariot.

April cold and wet fills barn and barrel.

So remember; when you see clouds upon the hills, you don't see clouds at all but crowds of daffodils; and when it rains it's not raining rain, you know. It's raining violets.

MAY

The sullen winter nearly spent,
Queen Flora to her garden went,
To call the flowers from their long sleep,
The year's glad festivals to keep.
   -- Ovid

One of the many festivals celebrated by the ancient Romans straddled the first day of May. This fertility festival, dedicated to Flora, the goddess who brought the fields and gardens to bloom each spring, subsequently evolved into May Day -- a holiday observed throughout Europe and brought to North America by the otherwise dour pilgrims.

Apparently the original concept of May Day got lost in the translation by the time it reached the British Isles. The Irish believed that spirits or fairies fought with each other and stole the best grain from the fields during this time of seasonal transition. On the Isles of Man and Manx they set bonfires on hilltops and children placed primroses at doorsteps to ward off the underworld spirits.

In most places, however, May Day represented an occasion for celebration and revelry. Young men and women in Scotland and England spent most of May Day Eve "bringing in the May" by gathering blooming branches from the forest and erecting a Maypole.

Of the varying customs that accompany May Day, the Maypole, seems the most prevalent. The earliest Maypole, a tree, felled and limbed of all but its topmost branches, symbolized the spirit of life in vegetation and probably derived from the pagan German belief that trees were sacred.

Trust not a day
Ere birth of May.
   -- Luther

In many temperate lands, "The merry month of May" heralds the end, at last, of cold weather and true summer begins. The farmer, however, has ambiguous feelings about May weather.

Blossoms in May
Are not good, some say.

May wet
Was never kind yet.

A wet May
Will fill a byre full of hay.

A cold May
Is good for corn and hay.

Cold May enriches no one.

JUNE

Officially, summer arrives on or about June 21st. No saints claim this auspicious occasion for their birthday. Consequently, lore must content itself with the Saints Medard (8th), Barnabas (11th), Vitus (15th), Protais (19th) and John (24th) to predict conditions for the coming summer.

If it rain on June 8th (St. Medard), it will rain forty days later; but if it rain on June 19th (St. Protais), it rains for forty days after.

On Saint Barnabas' Day
The sun is come to stay.

If Saint Vitus' Day be rainy weather,
It will rain for thirty days together.

Rain on Saint John's Day and we may expect a wet harvest.

JULY

July, God send thee calm and fayre,
    That happy harvest we may see,
With quyet tyme and healthsome ayre,
    And man to God may thankful bee.

Many Mediaeval peasants did not even own a calendar. Thanks to the clergy, however, they always knew the pending Saints days. Thus the lore of the Middle Ages tended to focus on and around these familiar days.

No fewer than seven July Saints rule the weather for the coming summer. One would hate to see rain on July 4th (Saint Martin Bullion's Day), July 15th (Saint Gallo's Day *and* Satin Swithin's Day), July 26th (Saint Anne's Day) or July 27th (Saint Godelieve's Day). Rain on any of these days promises 40 more days of continuous rain.

Apparently church officials decided at one time to move the popular Saint Swithin's remains from a lowly churchyard grave to holy ground. But a huge storm came up and persisted until the officials abandoned the idea. Lore thus attributes Saint Swithin with a powerful sway over weather. The weather on His Day, rain or fair, determines the weather for the coming 40 days.

Rain on Saint Mary's Day (July 2) promises only 30 more days of the same, but just a few puffy white clouds on Saint Jacob's Day (July 25th) "foretells much snow in the coming winter."

AUGUST

The English winter -- ending in July,
To recommence in August.
    -- Lord Byron

Lord Byron's gloomy take on the English winter does not reflect the general tenor of August weather lore. August, basically a fair month, does little or no harm to the harvest.

Dry August and warm,
Doth harvest no harm.

August sunshine and bright nights ripen the grapes.

When it rains in August, it rains honey and wine.

A wet August never brings dearth.

The days near the end of August often foretell the weather for the coming winter. Saint Bartholomew's day (August 24th) seems especially portentous.

As Saint Bartholomew's Day, so the whole autumn.

If it rains this day, it will rain the forty days after.

If the 24th of August be fair and clear,
Then hope for a prosperous autumn that year.

September

Saint Matthew, born on September 21st, makes the days and nights equal. The three days surrounding his birthday -- the autumnal equinox -- rule the weather for the entire season. A bountiful south wind on his day indicates that the rest of the autumn will be warm.
However,

Saint Matthew's rain fattens pigs and goats.

Matthews's Day, bright and clear,
Brings good wine in the next year.

In general, if "the storms in September clear off warm, all the storms of the following winter will be warm."

OCTOBER

In the summer, the earth stores a great deal of heat in the ground and in large bodies of water. This stored heat warms the winter winds as they push southward in the fall. Conversely, the earth runs a heat deficit during winter when the surface freezes. The stored cold cools the warm spring winds blowing from the south and delays summer. Because of this "thermal lag," autumns feel more like summer than winter and springs feel more like winter than summer.

If October bring much frost and wind, then are January and February mild.

Warm October, cold February.

As the weather in October, so will it be in the next March.

The northeast United States, during the mid or late autumn, often experiences a "season" called "Indian Summer" -- a delightful period of exceptionally warm sunny days that interrupt the gradual progression to colder weather expected in October and November. While other regions may also experience an extended summer or a warm fall, a true Indian Summer only occurs in the northern latitudes. At least one killing frost and, usually, a substantial period of normally cool weather precedes the occasion.

The phenomenon also occurs in England where, depending upon dates of occurrence, they call the event St. Martins summer, St. Lukes little summer, All-hallown summer, or poetically, the halcyon days.

There is often about this time a spell of fine, dry weather,
And this has received the name of Saint Lukes little summer.

There are always nineteen fine days in October.

NOVEMBER

No warmth, no cheerfulness, no healthful ease,
No comfortable feel in any member,
No shade, no shine, no butterflies, no bees,
No fruits, no flowers, no leaves, no birds,
No--vember.

November, a bleak month wherein people begin final preparations for winter -- and look forward to spring. They note especially the wind direction on Saint Martins day.

Wind northwest at Martinmas, severe winter to come.

If the wind is in the southwest at Martinmas, it keeps there till after Candlemas, with a mild winter up to then and no snow to speak of.

At Saint Martin's day
Winter is on his way.

DECEMBER

Saint Thomas, born on a winter solstice day, bears the responsibility for 28 days of subsequent weather.

Look at the weather cock on Saint Thomas' Day at twelve o'clock, and see which way the wind is, for there it will stick for the next (lunar) quarter.

According to lore, the period between December 25th and January 5th held the key for weather for the ensuing year.

If it rain much during the twelve days after Christmas, it will be a wet year.

Thunder during Christmas week indicates that there will be much snow during the winter.

A windy Christmas and a calm Candlemas are signs of a good year.

A clear and bright sun on Christmas Day fortelleth a peaceable year and plenty; but if the wind grow stormy before sunset, it betokeneth sickness in the spring and autumn quarters.

If Christmas Day on Thursday be,
A windy winter ye shall see;
Windy weather in each week,
And hard tempest strong and thick,
The summer shall be good and dry,
Corn and beasts shall multiply; . . .

New Year's Eve. What better time to check the weather for the coming year.

If New Year's Eve night wind blow south,
It betokens warmth and growth;
If west, much milk and fish in the sea;
If north, much cold and storms there will be;
If east, the trees will bear much fruit;
If northeast, flee it man and brute.

DOGS (AND OTHER WEATHER FORECASTERS)

DOG DAYS AND DOG FORECASTS

In ancient Greece and Rome, Dog Days began in early June when the Dog Star, Sirius, appeared at sunrise -- the helical rising of Sirius. The ancients held the star responsible for summer's heat blaming it for the hot dry weather in Athens, as well as the sultry days in Rome. In their eyes, the star caused wilting vegetation, human enervation, and exerted a baleful effect on all human affairs. The precession of the earth's axis has shifted the helical rising of Sirius -- and thus the dreaded Dog days -- to mid-July.

Dog days bright and clear
Indicate a happy year;
But when accompanied by rain,
For better times our hopes are vain.

If it rains on the first dog day, it will rain for forty days after.

As the dog days commence, so they end.

We now believe that during The Dog Days, a four to six weeks period between mid-July and early September (early July to the eleventh of August in western Europe) dogs go mad with the heat. In the southeastern United States, Dog Day weather may extend from mid-May to nearly October.

Dogs apparently excelled as weather forecasters in the Olden Days. Just about everything dogs did indicated an approaching storm. If they howled, dug holes, ate grass, became drowsy, rolled around and scratched, or just stretched out and slept, it presaged rain. To wit:

The unusual howling of dogs portends a storm.

Dogs making holes in the ground, howling when any one goes out, eating grass in the morning, or refusing meat, are said to indicate coming rain.

When dogs eat grass, it will be rainy.

If dogs roll on the ground and scratch, or become drowsy and stupid, it is a sign of rain.

If spaniels sleep more than usual, it foretells wet weather.

Sign, too, of rain: his outstretched feet the hound
Extends, and curves his belly to the ground.

AND CATS

Cats with their tails up and apparently electrified indicate approaching wind -- or a dog.

When the cat scratches the table legs, a change is coming.

Cats are observed to scratch the wall or a post before wind, and to wash their faces before a thaw; They sit with their backs to the fire before snow.

While rain depends, the pensive cat gives o'er
Her frolics, and pursues her tail no more.

AND GOATS?

According to a Scottish proverb,

Goats leave the high grounds and seek shelter before a storm.

But not just in Scotland. Roseburg, Oregon, once harbored a famous herd of prognosticating goats. Accounts of their forecasting feats appeared in various magazines and newspapers and David Brinkley once featured them on The Nightly News.

When the goats climbed the slopes of nearby Mt. Nebo to graze, the story goes, locals expected fair and dry weather. Goats foraging low on the hillside indicated a spell of inclement weather in the near future.

Rosenburg residents routinely relied on the goats location rather than the National Weather Service forecast because the goats maintained a 90 percent forecasting accuracy whereas the Weather Service could claim only 65 percent. A local radio station routinely issued Goat Weather Forecasts.

Unfortunately, the goats often behaved in unmannerly ways. Frequently they wandered into back yards and onto highways becoming both public nuisances and safety hazards. Roseburg citizens finally decided that problems caused by the wandering goats outweighed the advantage of accurate weather forecasts. They rounded up the entire herd and shipped it off to a nearby farm putting an abrupt end to its distinguished career in weather forecasting.

Flatlanders in need of accurate weather forecasts might consider the equally skilled sheep. Sheep have an advantage over goats in that they possess a less rambunctious temperament and require no mountain. Everything a sheep does presages rain. If they:

. . . turn their backs towards the wind, and remain so for some time, wet and windy weather is coming.

. . . gambol and fight, or retire to shelter, it presages a change in the weather.

. . . bleat much in the evening and during the night, severe weather is expected.

. . . quit their pastures with reluctance, it will rain the next day.

. . . eat greedily or . . . become frisky, leap and butt or 'box' each other . . . expect a storm.

OTHER ANIMALS

Naturalists as well as early shepherds and herdsmen have long attributed to animals an uncanny ability to sense approaching changes in the weather. In the annals of weather lore, many animals -- horses, asses, cows, bulls, sheep, goats, pigs, wolves, beavers, rats, mice, moles, rabbits, squirrels, weasels, hedgehogs, bats, all kinds of birds, and even fish -- seem endowed with an uncanny ability to sense minute changes in the atmosphere. Often they become unusually restless, return to their homes, eat avidity and, in general, exhibit unusual forms of behavior just before a storm.

ALMANACS

The word, "almanac" comes from Arabia and means "calendar of the skies." Since first devised by the Egyptians around 3000 B.C., almanacs have served as repositories of astronomical observations, principal holidays and important weather information.

In the beginning, ancient almanac makers provided movements of the planets, stars, sun, moon, and predictions of eclipses. Eventually, however, they went beyond mere timetables. Astrologers began to relate heavenly happenings to the events of man. Other groups added designated cultural and religious days, and linked the time to sow and reap specific crops with the appearance of certain star formations.

The Romans put their almanacs on blocks of wood measuring eight inches by two inches by two inches. They placed the astronomical timetables on one side and significant corresponding events on an adjoining side. These "clog" almanacs continued in use in the British Isles well into the 17th century.

At a time when no dependable calendar but the stars existed, Middle Age farmers and mariners found the almanac vital to their activities. Christopher Columbus navigated his way to the New World using an early German almanac for guidance.

American almanacs, of which hundreds have appeared over the years, assumed the role magazines later played and contributed significantly to our cultural development. In 1639, the American press printed its first two pieces of literature -- the *Freeman's Oath* followed by *An Almanac Calculated for New England*. Settlers, who depended on these books, took the proffered advice to heart and bought almanacs in quantities second only to Bibles. In addition to astrological charts, they included weather advice, native humor, down-home aphorisms and Calvinistic preachments designed to bolster hard working citizens to greater effort.

Ben Franklin, under the pseudonym Richard Saunders, printed his *Poor Richard's Almanack* from 1728 through 1753. Others continued to print *Poor Richard's* until 1796. As the archetype of American almanacs, it contained, in addition to a calendar and a weather forecast for the year, amusing stories, jokes and proverbs that attacked laziness, waste, avarice, and the other mortal sins of the age.

Franklin reworked the traditional European proverbs, casting them into an American context when necessary, and embedded permanently into the minds of generations of young children sayings such as;

Early to bed, early to rise, makes a man healthy, wealthy and wise.

A penny saved is a penny earned.

God helps those who help themselves.

Work as if you were to live a hundred years,
Pray as if you were to die tomorrow.

Over the centuries hundreds of such almanacs have brought timely information to the public. *Poor Robin's Almanac* of 1733 offered this bit of advice.

Observe which way the hedgehog builds her nest,
To front the north or south, or east or west;
For it 'tis true what common people say,
The wind will blow the quite contrary way.
If by some secret art the hedgehog knows,
So long before, the way in which the winds will blow,
She has an art which many a person lacks
That thinks himself fit to make our almanacs.

Judging from a passage from the *Old Farmer's Almanac* of 1763, almanac makers realized the shortcomings of their weather forecasts and treated the subject somewhat lightheartedly.

The Devil does not know so much of future events, as many expect an almanac maker should foretell; although it must be owned that they are willing to allow him the help of the Devil for his information.

Readers often joined in the fun and, recognizing the inherent inaccuracy of long-range weather forecasts, produced many versions of the "weather joke." i.e.

In one town, a youth could predict the weather with uncanny accuracy. When asked how he accomplished this, he said that he read the almanac and simply predicted the opposite of whatever it predicted for the day.

Robert B. Thomas's *Old Farmers Almanac* holds the record for longest continuous publication of an almanac. It first appeared in 1792 as *The Farmer's Almanack . . . for the Year of Our Lord 1793* and continues today as

The Old Farmers Almanac. Millions of Americans still consult it for its mixture of practical advice and entertainment -- and its long-range forecasts. The current version contains, "besides the large number of Astronomical Calculations and the Farmers Calendar for every month in the year, a variety of NEW, USEFUL, AND ENTERTAINING MATTER."

The "Farmers Calendar" divides the nation into 16 homogeneous climatic regions and forecasts the weather for each month for each of the 16 regions. The editors, employing a combination of "modern scientific methods," ancient weather wisdom, and a perfectly straight face, claim an accuracy of 80 percent.

AN ALL-ENCOMPASSING BIT 'O LORE

The hollow winds begin to blow,
The clouds look blank, the grass is low;
The soot falls down, the spaniels sleep,
The spiders from their cobwebs peep.
Last night the sun went pale to bed,
The moon's halos hid her head;
The boding shepherd heaves a sigh,
For see, a rainbow spans the sky.
The walls are damp, the ditches small,
Closed is the pink-eyed pimpernel.
Hark how the chairs and tables crack!
Old Betty's nerves are on the rack;
Loud quacks the duck, the peacocks cry,
The distant hills are seeming nigh,
How restless are the snorting swine,
The busy flies disturb the kine,
Low o'er the grass the swallow wings,
The cricket too, how sharp he sings!
Puss on the hearth, with velvet paws,
Sits wiping o'er her whiskered jaws;
Through the clear streams the fishes rise,
And nimbly catch the incautious flies.
The glow worms, numerous and light,

Illumined the dewy dell last night;
At dusk the squalid toad was seen,
Hopping and crawling o'er the green;
The whirling dust the wind obeys,
And in the rapid eddy plays;
The frog has changed his yellow vest,
And in a russet coat is dressed.
Though June, the air is cold and still,
The merry blackbirds voice is shrill;
My dog, so altered in his taste,
Quits mutton bones on grass to feast;
And see yon rooks, how odd their flight!
They imitate the gliding kite,
And seem precipitate to fall,
As if they felt the piercing ball.
'T will surely rain; I see with sorrow,
Our jaunt must be put off to-morrow.
      -- Dr. Edward Jenner

And rain it surely must. Should even half of these indicators occur, a cold front will soon arrive.

REFERENCES

Allègre, Claude, *The Behavior of the Earth -- Continental and Seafloor Mobility*, Harvard University Press, 1988

Alley, Richard B. and Michael L. Bender, *Greenland Ice Cores, Frozen in Time*, Scientific American, February 1998, pp 80

Allman, William F. and Betsy Wagner, *Climate and the Rise of Man*, U.S. News and World Report, June 8, 1992

Andrews, Antony, *The Greeks*, Norton & Co., 1967

Asimov, Isaac, *Biographical Encyclopedia of Science and Technology*, Doubleday, 1982

Asimov, Isaac, *How Did We Find Out About the Atmosphere*, Walker & Co., 1985

Asimov, Isaac, *Beginnings, The Story of Origins . . .*, Berkley Books, 1989

Barnett, Mary, *Gods and Myths of Ancient Greece*, Smithmark, 1996

Bates, Robert L. and Julia A. Jackson, *Dictionary of Geological Terms*, Anchor Books, 1984

Bordaz, Jacques, *Tools of the Old and New Stone Age*, Dover Publications, 1989

Bowra, C. M., *The Greek Experience*, Mentor Books, 1963

Brander, Bruce, *The River Nile*, National Geographic Society, 1966 (a book)

Burn, A.R., *The Pelican History of Greece*, Penguin Books, 1965

Butzer, Karl W., *The Sahara and Eastern Africa during the Late Pleistocene, Environment and Archeology*, Aldine Publishing Co., 1964

Butzer, Karl W., *Climate Changes in the Arid Zones of Africa during early to mid-Holocene Times*, In World Climate from 8000 to 0 B.C., Proceedings of the International Symposium, London, April, 1966, RMS Publication

Calvin, William H., *The Emergence of Intelligence*, Scientific American, Oct. 1994

Cambridge Encyclopedia of Human Evolution, *The Dispersion of Modern Humans*, PP395

Caputo, Robert, *Journey Up the Nile*, National Geographic, May, 1985

Carson, Rachel, *Silent Spring*, Houghton Miffin, May, 1962

Copleston, Frederick, *A History of Philosophy*, Book 1, Doubleday, 1985

Crawford, Michael and David Marsh, *The Driving Force, Food, Evolution and the Future*, Harper & Row, 1989

Davidson, Keay and A. R. Williams, *Hot Theories on the Center of the Earth*, National Geographic, Jan, 1995

Dawson, Alastair G., *Ice Age Earth -- Late Quaternary Geology and Climate*, Routledge, 1994

Demillo, Rob, *How Weather Works*, Zif--Davis Press, 1994

Dickerson, Richard E., *Chemical Evolution and the Origin of Life*, Scientific American, September, 1978

Doren, Charles Van, *A History of Knowledge*, Balentine Books, 1991

Dott, Robert H., and Roger LO. Batten, *Evolution of the Earth*, McGraw-Hill, 1988

Dutton, John A., *The Ceaseless Wind*, Dover Publications, Inc., 1986

Erickson, Jon, *The Living Earth*, TAB books, 1989

Erickson, Jon, *Glacial Geology*, Facts on File, Inc., 1996

ESSA Magazine, *Centennial of the U.S. Weather Service*, January, 1970

Fortey, Richard, *Life*, Alfred A Knopf, 1998

Frakes, L. A., *Climates Throughout Geological Time*, Elsevier Scientific Publishing Co., 1979

Freier, George D., *Weather Proverbs*, Fisher Books, 1992

Garraty, John A. and Peter Gay (Ed.), *The Columbia History of the World*, Harper & Row,1981

Gedzelman, Staney David, *Beyond Bergan*, Weatherwise, June, 1995

Gedzelman, Staney David, *Automating the Atmosphere*, Weatherwise, June, 1995

Gleick, James, Chaos, *Making a New Science*, Vicking Penguin Books, 1987

Gordon, Cyrus H., *The Ancient Near East*, Norton & Company, 1958

Gore, Rick, *The Dawn of Humans -- Neanderthals*, National Geographic, January, 1996

Gore, Rick, *The Dawn of Humans -- Tracking the First of Our Kind*, National Geographic, September, 1997

Gould, Stephen Jay, *Ever Since Darwin -- Reflections in Natural History*, W. W. Norton & Co., 1977

Graedel, Thomas E. and Paul J. Crutzen, *Atmosphere, Climate, and Change*, Scientific American Library, 1995

Ferring, C. Reid, *The Aterian in North African Prehistory*, in Problems in Prehistory: North Africa and the Levant, Southern Methodist University, 197?

Hamilton, Edith, *Mythology*, Little Brown & Co., 1942

Hamilton, Edith, *The Greek Way*, W. W. Norton & Co., 1942

Hamyln, D. W., *Western Philosophy*, Penguin Books, 1987

Harding, A. F. (ed), *Climate Change in Later Pre-History*, Edinburgh University Press, 1982 (Bintliff, J. L.)

Harper Collins, Past Worlds; *An Atlas of Archaeology*, Harper--Collins, 1989

Hawkes, Jacquetta, *The Atlas of Early Man*, St. Martin's Press, New York, 1976

Hazen, Robert M. and James Trefil, *Science Matters -- Achieving Scientific Literacy*, Anchor Books, 1991

Hillel, Daniel, *Out of the Earth, Civilization and the Life of the Soil*, University of California Press, 1992

Holford, Ingrid, *The Guinness Book of Weather Facts & Feats*, Guiness, 1977

Hope, Murry, *The Elements of the Greek Tradition*, Element Books, England

Hoyle, Fred, *Ice -- The Ultimate Human Catastrophe*, The Continuum Publishing Co., 1981

Hyams, Edward, *Soil & Civilization*, Harper and Row, 1976

Horstmeyer, Steve, *A Trip to the Ice*, Weatherwise, June/July 1993

Hughes, Patrick, *Mythical Meteorology*, ESSA Magazine, January, 1970

Hughes, Patrick, *Early American Weathermen*, ESSA Magazine, April, 1970

Hughes, Partick, *A Century of Weather Service*, Gordon and Breach, 1970

Hughes, Patrick, *Children of the Cold*, Weatherwise, Dec '93/Jan '94

Hughes, Patrick, *The New Meteorology*, Weatherwise, June, 1995

Hughes, Patrick, *Winning the War*, Weatherwise, June, 1995

Hughes, Patrick, *Realizing the Digital Dream*, Weatherwise, June, 1995

Inwards, Richard, *Weather Lore*, London, 18??

Imbrie, John and Katherine Palmer Imbrie, *Ice Ages, Solving the Mystery*, Harvard University Press, 1994

Johnson, Donald and Maitland Edey, *Lucy*, University of Chicago Magazine, Spring, 1981

Kerr, Richard A., *The Greatest Extinction Gets Greater*, Science, Vol. 262, 26 Nov. 1993

Kitto, H.D., *The Greeks*, Penguin Books, 1951

Kinder, Hermann and Werner Kilgemann, *The Anchor Atlas of World History*, Vol I, Anchor Books, 1974

Krupp, Edwin C., Echoes of the Ancient Skies, *The Astronomy of Lost Civilizations*, Oxford University Press, 1983

Kuhn, Thomas S., *The Structure of Scientific Revolutions*, University of Chicago Press, 1970

Kutzbach, Gisela, *The Thermal History of Cyclones, A History of Meteorological Thought in the 19th Century*, American Meteorological Society, 1979

Lafferty, Peter, *Weather -- Science Facts*, Crescent Books, New York, 1992

Lamb, H. H., *On the Nature of Certain Climatic Epochs which Differed from the Modern Normal*, Proceedings, WMO -- UNESCO Symposium of Climate Changes, Rome, 1961 -- UNESCO Arid Zone Research, 20: 120-150

Lambert, David, *The Field Guide to Early Man*, The Diagram Group, 1987

Laskin, David, *Braving the Elements, The Stormy History of American Weather*, Doubleday, 1996

Lee, Albert, *Weather Wisdom, Facts and Folklore of Weather Forecasting*, Gongdon & Weed, 1976

Lewin, Roger, *In the Age of Mankind*, Smithsonian Books, 1988

Lieberman, Philip, *Uniquely Human*, Harvard University Press, 1991

Lovelock, James, *The Ages of Gaia*, A Biography of Our Living Earth, Norton & Company, 1995

Lorenz, Edward, *The Essence of Chaos*, University of Washington Press, 1995

Ludlum, David, *The Weather Factor*, Houghton Mifflin, 1984

Lyons, Walter A., *The Handy Weather Answer Book*, Visible Ink Press, 1997

Marks, Anthony E., *The Current Status of the Upper Paleolithic Studies from the Maghreb to the Northern Levant*, (in) Problems in Pre-History -- North Africa and the Levant, Southern Methodist University Press, 1975

Mayall, R. Newton and Margaret W. Mayall, *Sundials*, Third Edition, Sky Publishing, 1994

McSween, Harry Y., Jr., *Stardust to Planets*, St. Martins Press, 1993

Monastersky, Richard, *Staggering through the Ice Ages*, Science News, Vol. 146, July 30, 1994

Monastersky, Richard, *New Beat Detected in the Ice Age Rhythm*, Science News, Vol. 147, Feb. 25, 1995

Nicholson, S. E., *Climate and History*, Wigley, Ingram and Farmer, 1981

National Museum of Natural History, *Ice Age Mammals and the Emergence of Man*, Elephant Press

Nesme-Ribes, Elizabeth, Sallie L. Baliunas and Dmitry Sokoloff, *The Stellar Dynamo*, Scientific American, August, 1996

Newton, Chester W. and Eero O. Holopainen, *Extratropical Cyclones -- The Erik Palmén Memorial Volume*, American Meteorological Society, Boston, 1990

O'Connor, D. J., *A Critical History of Western Philosophy*, The Free Press (Macmillan), 1964

Pearce, E. A. and C. G. Smith, *The Times Books World Weather Guide*, Times Books, 1984

Pokras, Edward M., *Pliocene History of South Saharan/Sahelian Aridity*, (Columbia University Press), 199?

Raymo, Chet, *Biography of a Planet*, Prentice-Hall, 1984

Reifsnyder, William E., *Weathering the Wilderness*, The Sierra Club Guide to Practical Meteorology, Sierra Club Books, 1980

Riley, Denis and Lewis Spolton, *World Weather and Climate*, Chambridge Univ. Press, 1981

Sagan, Carl and Ann Druyan, *Shadows of Forgotten Ancestors*, 1992, Ballantine Books, New York

Sahakian, William S., *History of Philosophy*, Barnes and Noble Outline Series, 1968

Sampson, Russell D., *Jewels of the Sky*, Earth Magazine, October, 1996

Sanders, Ti, Weather: *A User's Guide to the Atmosphere*, Icarus Press, South Bend, Indiana, 1985

Saucier, Walter J., *Principles of Meteorological Analysis,* Dover Publications, 1989

Sawyer, J.S., Possible Variation of the General Circulation of the Atmosphere, World Climate from 8000 to 0 B.C., Proceedings of the International Symposium, London, April, 1966, RMS Publication

Schaefer, Vincent J. and John A. Day, *Atmosphere*, Peterson Field Guides, Houghton Mifflin, 1981

Schneider, Stephan H. and Randi Londer, *The Co-evolution of Climate and Life*, Sierra Club Books, 1984

Schopf, J. William, *The Evolution of the Earliest Cells*, Scientific American, September, 1978

Science News, *From Proteins to Protolife*, Vol. 146, July 23, 1994

Selby, M. J., *Pluvials in Northern and Eastern Africa and Their Relations to Glacial Climates in Europe*, Environmental Studies, University of Witwatersrand, 1977

Shreeve, James, *The Neanderthal Peace*, Discovery Magazine, September, 1995

Stanley, Steven M., *Earth and Life Through Time*, 2nd Ed., W.H. Freeman & Co., New York, 1989

Stevens, William K., *Life in the Stone Age: New Finding Point to Complex Societies*, The New York Times, December 20, 1988

Suplee, Curt, *Untangling the Science of Climate*, National Geographic, May 1998

Tannahill, Reay, *Food in History*, Stein and Day, New York, 1973

Tabruck, Edward J. and Fredrick K. Lutgens, *Earth Science*, 1991, Macmillion Publishing Co., New York

Tattersal, Ian, *The Human Odyssey*, Four Million Years of Human Evolution, Prentice Hall, 1993

Valentine, James W., *The Evolution of multicellular Plants and Animals*, Scientific American, September, 1978

Walker, Alan and Pat Shipman, *The Wisdom of the Bones*, Alfred A. Knopf, 1996

Washburn, Sherwood, L., *The Evolution of Man*, Scientific American, Sept. 1978

Watson, Benjamin A. and Editors of The Old Farmers Almanac, *The Old Farmers Almanac Book of Weather & Natural Disasters*, Random House, 1993

Watson, Lyall, *Heaven's Breath, A Natural History of the Wind*, Hodder and Stoughton, 1984

Wenforf, F. and A. E. Marks (ed.), *Problems in Prehistory -- North Africa and the Levant*, Southern Methodist University Press, 1975

Westbroek, Peter, *Life as a Geological Force*, W.W. Norton & Co., New York/London, 1991

Williams, Jack, *The Weather Book*, Vintage Books, 1992

McWilliams, Brenden, *Weather Eye*, The Lilliput Press, 1994

INDEX

A

air mass/polar front theory, 74
Alberta Clipper, 71
Almanacs, 186
Anemometer, 52
Asia, 17, 20, 26, 28, 30, 31, 37, 39, 40, 45,
    70, 145
asthenosphere, 1, 11, 12
Atmospheric Chemistry, 154
Australia, 128
Austria, 128
autumnal equinox, 134, 141, 180
axis of rotation, 92, 125, 132, 133, 134,
    135, 141, 142, 153
Azores High, 17

B

Babylonians, 146
Barometer, 49
Beaufort Wind Scale, 165
Beijing, 30
biosphere, 10, 11, 12, 13, 16, 63, 64, 136,
    139, 140
Bjerknes-Bergen model, 73
Boyle, Robert, 50, 61, 63, 64, 78, 82
Boyle-Mariotte gas law, 63
Brazil, 113

C

California, 105, 158, 193
Canada, 3, 71, 128, 158
carbon dioxide (CO_2), 3, 6, 7, 8, 9, 10, 13,
    122, 123, 124, 144, 153
Celcius, Anders, 51
Chad, 19, 20, 22
China, 18, 27, 120, 122
chinook, 159
Christians, 44
cirrostratus, 151
cirrus clouds, 87, 149
Civil War, 70, 168
climate changes, 1, 3, 115, 139, 140, 154
climate controls, xiii
Climatology, xii, xiii
Columbus, Christopher, 187
continental drift, 12, 115, 137, 153
Copernicus, 147
copper, 55
Coriolis Force, 23
corona, 149, 151
Cro-Magnon Man, 29
cryosphere, 136, 140
cup anemometer, 52
cyanobacteria, 9
cyclogenesis, 22, 86, 98, 100, 107, 109

D

da Vinci, Leonardo, 51